Mansfield.

Running Wild

It was Peggy who painted the black cat green, who could not resist the most beautiful flower in the Angry Woman's garden, who released Georgie's captive butterflies, and was caught playing with Riki in her bedroom at dawn ... The events and emotions that were landmarks in the childhood of the youngest member of a large family are vividly recalled in an appealing autobiographical story by one of today's major illustrators, and drawn with a fine sensitivity.

RUNNING WILD

Written and Illustrated by
PEGGY FORTNUM

CHATTO & WINDUS · LONDON

Published by
Chatto & Windus Ltd
42 William IV Street
London WC2N 4 DF

*

Clarke, Irwin & Co. Ltd
Toronto

Text and illustrations © Peggy Fortnum 1975

ISBN 0 7011 5068 8

All rights reserved. No part of this publication may be reproduced, stored in a retrieval system, or transmitted in any form, or by any means, electronic, mechanical, photocopying, recording or otherwise, without the prior permission of Chatto & Windus Ltd.

Printed in Great Britain by
Northumberland Press Ltd, Gateshead

Contents

HESTER	11
THE GREEN CAT	23
THE ANGRY WOMAN	35
THE WEDDING	47
IN THE DARK	61
THE TRAP	73
THE VILLAGE	83
QUICKSANDS	95
CHRISTMAS	113
THE QUARREL	121
THE POEM	131
THE PICNIC	141

FOR RALPH

Hester

"I don't know what I would have done without Hester," my mother often used to say, "she had a way with babies."

It was a well-known fact, in our family, that a baby stopped crying as soon as Hester picked it up, and stayed from there on in a state of contentment.

As I was the youngest of six children, and born in my mother's fortieth year, by the time I could walk, all my brothers and sisters looked grown-up to me, and I lived and felt like an only child. I would have been more solitary if it had not been for Hester who was a shy young country girl my mother had engaged as a much needed help in the house. Later she had come to live with us.

Hester was as gentle as a nice day in summer, and as calm, with her air of serenity and being at peace with everything. She had, however, a melancholy side which I sensed in her sad thin singing, and in an occasional rapt and contemplative stare. In these moods she would reply to even a trivial question in a repetitive way, turning her sparse vocabulary into a significant and dramatic utterance.

"Oh no, dear! I would never do that," she might say. "Oh no, dear! Never, never, dear! I would never do that, dear, no!"

When I was old enough to notice, I would occasionally see her standing at the window and looking out, as if waiting, or listening to a voice that no one else could hear. Someone tried to explain her tranquillity by saying, "She must have seen a vision and never got over it." Whatever the cause, as a child, it was sufficient to experience the effect. She was never unkind or angry or even irritable with me; and I must have been an irritating child. I was up in the air with excitement one minute, and down in the dumps in the next. I was unpunctual for meals, and generally missing at the end of the day, and had to be sought for by some protesting member of the family who considered they had more important things to do. My eldest brother Ranald was working in South Africa, and reappeared only to get married. My sister Toddy had also married, and apart from an occasional holiday with us, lived in Scotland with her husband. Being so young I did not notice their absence, and the house still seemed to be full of brothers and sisters rushing about on what appeared to me to be grown-up affairs. They tramped up and downstairs in school boots or tripped about in fancy-dress clothes. They fought, quarrelled, laughed, shouted, whispered, giggled and sang. My other sister Niña was constantly practising on the piano, when she was not drawing or giving little parties for her student friends; and I used to watch them dancing something they called "The Charleston" to a high-pitched fidgety kind of music on a screechy gramophone that had a large convoluted horn.

Finding myself excluded from their activities, I would inevitably wander downstairs to the basement to look for Hester, who, in all the ups and downs of our family life remained unshaken like a rock in a rough sea. She was my refuge: but the whole kitchen was like a cave, with the flames snapping in the stove, and the white plates shining like full moons. In the scullery the washing bubbled in the copper boiler, and was carried out in large wicker baskets to be hung between the pear trees. Running outside I would be dazzled by the sight of sheets tossing in the sky, petals flying in the wind, and Hester's apron like a balloon.

Tea was the best meal of the day, and I had it with Hester in the kitchen. I sat with her at a big wooden table, and ate thick slices of bread spread with dripping or sprinkled with brown sugar.

I suppose Hester might have been considered plain by some people. Her thin hair was scraped back in a tight little knot, and her face looked as if it had been carved in bone; otherwise there was nothing about her that reminded one of bone or tightness: her expression was generous, and her eyes were the colour of distant rain. Naturally I considered her to be a person of great beauty, and sometimes I made a point

of telling her so. I am not too certain that she knew what I meant, anyway she never replied. She would turn her cup slowly round and round in a circle, a little unconscious gesture she had, and look at me, or through me, as if she saw a star.

When I reached the age of five, my parents went out more often, particularly to the theatre, and Hester and I were often on our own. If it was summer, we went to visit Hester's mother, Mrs. Smith.

Running Wild

Mr. and Mrs. Smith lived in a cottage at South Harrow which at that time was still in the country, surrounded by meadows full of buttercups and barley. We took a bus from Harrow High Street which left us some fifteen minutes later standing on a grass bank near a singing telegraph pole. The air smelt sweet and clean, and the bushes were full of birds. The rough road leading to the cottage had a ditch on each side and a border of long grass thick with wild flowers. I was encouraged to pick a bunch for Mrs. Smith, while Hester told me some of their names: Shepherd's Purse, Old Man's Beard, Ragged Robin, Meadowsweet, Milkmaid, Speedwell, Ox-eye-daisy, and many others. By the time we got to the house, the bunches always drooped and were almost too big for me to hold.

Mrs. Smith was slight and gentle and as quiet as a little ghost. I can see her now, fading away from me, into the dark of the house; she must have gone to look for vases and jam-jars. Opposite the front door was another door which opened on to a staircase leading to the upstairs rooms. Downstairs there were rag rugs, ticking clocks, and pictures of people I cannot remember. But I was not observant in this way. This house was the end of a journey for me, which gave me a feeling of peace delightfully mixed with excitement.

I was left to brood in the garden without any feeling of loneliness, and I investigated its treasures with the same sense of fulfilment. The pond was still and clear, with a thick edge of forget-me-nots as blue as the sky. There was an iron hoop hanging on the wall which I could take down and bowl along with a stick. But I felt no need to play, to act, to run; there was a sense of listening in the garden which caught me spellbound. I watched the pond change from blue to black as the sun moved slowly behind the trees, and the trees turned upside-down in the water.

Later when I was called indoors, everything swam in a haze of tobacco smoke. I would see a large man with a great beard sitting at the head of a table in a small room which was full of the humming sound of talk. This was Mr. Smith. A carter by trade, he had eyes like sparks in a bush. To cool his tea he would pour it in a saucer and drink it with a satisfying, bubbling sound, all the while preparing a joke for me, which was usually one about flowers.

"Did you know," he would say, looking at me, "that a dandelion is an Irishman's buttercup?" Seeing my astonishment, laughter would rise from his chest and tremble round the table. I would draw back in my chair, between my protectors who were soft and leaning. They would give me bread and honey, and sometimes radishes, or a pat-a-cake biscuit. In later years Hester would chuckle at the thought of it. "We were always so surprised that you believed him," she said. But I could not help believing him; to me he was a giant; a kind of country god, with a knowledge that was indisputable.

By the time we arrived home it was usually dark and I was allowed to stay up late for a treat. The nights my parents were out I slept in Hester's room in the attic on the fourth floor. For once I was relieved of the agony of lying in a room on my own, listening to imaginary footsteps on the creaking stairs. At that time we had gaslights which popped and hummed uneasily on the landing and in the hall. But these were never used by Hester: a candle would be lit in the kitchen and we would start on a journey to the top of the house.

As we climbed the stairs, I watched the shadows spread like the wings of bats and the long rocking dark bars of the banisters walked on the wall by Hester's side. Any slight draught would blow the candle-flame backwards, and all the dark shapes round us would move in one massive night march upwards.

Once we reached our room, the shadows settled into the corners; the curtains were drawn, and the ceiling sloped protectively over our beds as we lay in the dark talking.

Outside the house I could hear the shuffle of leaves in the trees below, boys calling in the street, the distant throb of a bus, or a slow rumbling train. Hester's words wove in and out of these sounds, forming images which emerge now like some old story I seem to have heard in a dream.

"When I was small," said Hester, "it thundered, and Harriet hid in the cupboard saying, 'Why does God shout so loud?' But I told her that He did so to show happiness in all the things He made, which had to be rained upon before they could grow, and Harriet came out of the dark and played with the doll my father gave me.

"I watched at the window until the clouds had passed, and saw the gypsies come, and people locked their doors and turned away. But Father let them into all his fields, and even fetched the doctor for one of them. They were a strong lot for all that, and never minded storms, but picked cowslips while it rained when the buds were young. You should have seen the old farm! The apples we had ... the branches almost broke with the weight. They picked the lot while the weather lasted and sold for a good price.

"Then Father sent me to school and I wore boots. One day we all stood in front of the camera with our hair in ribbons. You remember the picture? It was in the book that had Mother and my sister Violet in it. I was the one at the end in a pinafore. I don't remember much about the school. I expect they were trying to be kind and couldn't help being what they were, but I was glad when I left and a nice old lady took me for ironing and said I was the best.

"They started building houses at that time, down the lane, and I thought, 'How nice, I'd like to have one in red brick.' I didn't want too much, because there is no need to have a lot, and then I met the lad who went fighting when the war came. He never wrote, not being much of a hand for it. But one day I saw him walking down the road looking fit and ... well! ... I went to meet him, just like we used to when the day was done and said, 'Hallo! You're

Hester

back, come and have a cup of tea.' I thought I saw him smile and come towards me. But what do you think! The road was empty, nothing but dust, and me walking and talking to myself. I must have been dreaming. I had a telegram the very day I saw him. They said he'd gone. So it is not all what one expects.

"Look at your mother, with your father out of work. When you were on the way, she said to me, 'Hester, you must go and get a better job.' But I said, 'Oh no, Ma'am, I love babies, I don't want the money.' So I stayed, and you arrived in time for Christmas when everyone expected presents. Master Derek didn't like it much, he wanted football boots. But Miss Niña said you were just what she needed, being the odd one out.

"They only had one toy each, and stockings of course, with chocolate buttons, a penny at the bottom, and oranges. Master Ranald was too old for that; so was Miss Toddy. Miss Niña hung up one of your daddy's socks, and got something she didn't want, so we gave her the crackers. Poor Master Derek hadn't got his football boots and Master David had a bad cold. Mrs Patterson gave us half a cake with a candle on it. The first to blow it out got the Father Christmas. We gave you an icing-sugar baby.

"Master David wanted to be an Indian, and had his way in the end. When your Daddy found him, he'd got as far as the Harrow Metropolitan line.

"Then we all sang 'Once in Royal David's City' round the piano; you never heard such a din; your father couldn't play a penny whistle for toffee apples.

"I remember the year the snow fell, as high as a hedge in some places and there wasn't coal enough to make a proper fire. It was a big day when your father went to London and got himself a job. He sat in a room all on his own, with good money I hear. 'But Hester,' he said, 'it's not like the sea. I could stand up there on a rough boat and be myself. Ship's biscuits had maggots in them, but there were compensations. I could follow the right star with a clear eye, and keep a steady head. What good is a compass locked in a drawer?' ... Even his sword was hanging on the wall, his name in gold; I saw it on a box one day in your mother's room—PRIZE, it said, MIDSUMMER 1889.

"Did you know that he could play the fiddle? Not that he had a bit of Scotch in him, or Irish. He was a plain farmer's son. Soft fruits, if I remember. You had a sweet Granny. When he was a child, he used to lick the cream off the top of the buckets of milk when no one was looking, and ride to school on a pony, until he ran away to sea and joined a ship. It was a hard life but he liked it. Sailing boats were big in those days, going by the pictures we had ... of waves ... whales spouting ... many lives were lost. His

Hester

brown eyes changed to blue—'From looking at the sea,' they said, 'such things can happen' ... But goodness! What am I thinking about, that was long ago. When he was older he took command, and sailed right through the war.

"It's my opinion, now I look back on it, that your father was all at sea and never noticed that your mother's face was getting thinner, saying it would pass, when I could see that she was drifting. With the March wind and the spring late in coming, the cold was in one's very bones.

"It was turn and turn about that night the Doctor came. I said to your father, 'I think we should have another opinion, I can see her sinking if something isn't done.' 'Hester, you're right,' he said, and sure enough, with two opinions, she was taken away with double pneumonia. 'Just in time,' I thought, 'another day would have been too late.' Not that she minded, poor soul, drifting off without a care. The Doctor kept shaking her arm saying, 'Think of your children, Mary, think of your baby.' It wakened her, and she put up a struggle.

"Do you remember not remembering your mother when we went to see her sitting up in bed at the Cottage Hospital?

"I had to sing praises—not that I ever saw angels at the Baptists. I only saw them once; one day on the hill ... You know the church, don't you? I saw them come in as clear as I see you ... What did you say, dear? Was it the sun coming through the windows? No dear, it wasn't the sun, it was angels. I well remember, as I hadn't thought to see them ... not that day I hadn't.

"'Home has changed, Hester,' your mother said, 'it all looks better than I thought.' Well, we'd spent the day washing it clean, and all the cups were laid and ready. With a silk shawl your father bought, and a fan from Fly—Fly was your mother's friend from Tobago—it was all as good as could be done. When your father found us making Dandy-Jim with cherries in it, he took your mother waltzing all round the kitchen table.

Running Wild

"A great thunderstorm raged that night, but the hill divided the storm, so all we got was a gentle rain, with the scent coming out of the trees, and everyone tired out from dancing, with your mother back, and you in your first frock with a rainbow ribbon round it ... your mother said she had never seen anything like it ... over the trees. Do you remember the candles shining ... round the room ..." Hester's voice seemed to be receding as I was getting sleepier ... "The moon came out in the end ... through the clouds. Do you remember ..." I could not remember anything and the room was getting comfortingly warm and black. "I remember the candles, and the tree and that good-night," said Hester, "but I think we had better go to sleep now, darling. Good-night, Peggy. Sleep ... sleep well." The room was at last silent.

Hester's words turned slowly round and round my drowsy mind, like some familiar dream I knew by heart. She seems to me now, rather like a bird that sings at the end of the day. Once her territory had been established, the boundaries of our home made clear, we would fold the bed-clothes over our heads and fall asleep.

The Green Cat

In the mornings I used to go shopping with my mother in the town, which lay at the foot of Harrow-on-the-Hill.

At the back of the shops there were tall trees, and paddocks, and playing fields, and horses with sweeping tails clopped lazily up and down the roads pulling carts. In the High Street there were open-top double-decker buses, where the passengers on the top deck had to hold up umbrellas when it rained. There were a lot of bicycles, a few cars, some delivery vans, and any number of hand-carts and hawkers' barrows. Nearly every day somebody would be standing at the side of the road selling something, such as balloons, kites, celluloid windmills, or fluffy toys that could be wound up with a key, and set running, and squeaking, or hopping about the pavement. More often than not there would be the sound of an organ-grinder, or a one-man band, and sometimes I saw a man in a swinging kilt playing the bag-pipes. I used to half hide behind my mother as he came towards us roaring with three horns snarling and whining, his great cloak swaying back and forth, and his legs like tree-trunks. On the whole it was a sufficiently big town for me to be impressed, and the people living in it were strange enough to rouse my curiosity. I tried to understand why they were living in the world—a question I had not yet applied to myself—and why they all looked so different to me and my family.

My large eyes may have worried my mother who warned me not to stare, particularly at a cripple, or a hunch-back, or anyone in any other way disfigured, for fear of hurting their feelings. This was difficult as I was amazed at first when I saw people walking past each other in the street, and I waited for them to smile or say, "It's you," or make some kind of sign to show that they knew we were there. Instead they behaved as if we were invisible, and their faces were blank as they walked right past us. I could not help telling my mother how I felt about this. "Wouldn't it be nice," I said, "if every time someone passed us in the street we talked, instead of pretending that we couldn't see each other?" "It would take up too much time," said my mother, who was hurrying along with a basket. I thought she was wrong, but after some consideration I had to agree with her, and in the end I got used to it.

When my mother had finished shopping she would buy me a bun or a sponge-cake finger or, if there was time, she would take me to a new place called Lyons, where I would sit at a marble-top table with gold legs, and a girl in a bright white apron and crown threaded with ribbon, would bring me a real strawberry ice in a silver cup with a long stem. Then my mother would go home to peel the potatoes and help Hester get the lunch.

In the afternoon I had nothing to do except play with my toys and explore the garden. I did not have any chalks or crayons at that time, so I could not draw, but I used to enjoy blowing bubbles out of a clay-pipe from a bowl of soapy water, hoping they would not burst as I watched them float away. I was beginning to be attracted by colours and shapes, which must have started one day when I was being pushed in a wheeled-chair by Hester's sister Pemmie. Pemmie also came part-time to "help out" and she was taking me for a walk in the recreation ground.

That particular day was a gloomy one, grey, with rain in the air, and I suddenly became very much aware of appearances. The recreation ground filled me with dejection and depression. In a melancholy trance, I contemplated its ugliness; that vast expanse of flat grass was like a never-ending desert; the trees at the side of the path were fenced in by a barrier of iron palings; and there was nothing else for me to see but a strip of short sour-looking grass and a few stunted, ragged daisies. Outside the recreation ground, I knew we would be passing rows and rows of houses all looking exactly like each other, and "bored—bored—bored" I would have said, if I had known the word, as the wheels rattled and clattered as they turned round and round down the concrete path.

The next minute, Pemmie had seen a flower growing through the paling, and picking it, she put it in my hands, where it blazed in front of me like a sun. The excitement roused in me by its shape and colour had stimulated my desire for activity. Something had to be done about this, but what? For lack of ideas, I found myself picking the petals off, one by one, and was left with a small knob on the end of a stalk. To my dismay I realised there was no way of getting them back. The gold had gone; the treasure was irretrievable. My stupidity at having spoilt something good to look at seemed to connect me in a depressing way with the landscape which I had found so ugly and uninteresting, and now I had made myself a part of it all.

This memory remained, and by the time I was four years old I was probably unconsciously trying to discover a way of recreating what I had lost.

I became familiar with a world of small things. Stones, snails, feathers, conkers, ladybirds, caterpillars, acorns; my sense of touch soon added to my enjoyment. The velvet skins on the nuts that fell from the almond tree. The slippery silk touch of leaves from the acacia which fell off smoothly like feather-weight pennies when I ran my fingers down one of the twigs. The watery cool stems of fresh cut grass.

My first creative experience arrived in an accidental way when I found a large tin of paint the decorators had left outside the back door with a brush beside it; the paint was green and looked creamy and inviting, and I might have stopped considering what to do with it if our cat had not come swaying down the path, slowly and deliberately as all cats do, then sat down in front of me and yawned.

Billy the cat was black. I tried to imagine what it must be like to be one colour all the time, and then I realised that Billy must be a bored cat; he had been black as long as I could remember, and spent most of the day sleeping. Any

Running Wild

attempts to get him to play with me were unsuccessful; he would raise a surprised head, frown with disgust, then patiently close his eyes again, expecting me to take the hint and go away. I wanted to do something for Billy that would renew his life and give him a fresh interest. It seemed far more important to decorate a living creature who could respond with pleasure, than to decorate an inanimate object that could not. So that was the day Billy became a green cat. Dripping little blobs of paint, he disappeared quickly into the house and as time went by more slowly when I was a child, I forgot all about it.

The next thing I remember is the uproar and the fuss. The sound of everyone talking at once confused me, and it was only gradually that I was able to connect the noise with the cat, the cat with the paint, and in the commotion that followed, the fact that nobody approved of what I had done. I stood about helplessly looking on while everyone, faced by an unusual event, tried to find a way of showing me the enormity of my offence and rescue Billy at the same time. "Oh! Peggy, how could you do such a thing?" was continually reiterated. Fortunately, they did not seem to expect

The Green Cat

an answer, as I could never have expressed my original idea in words. My voice, in any case, would have been lost in the kind of operatic storm that followed.

"He's run away, I can't find him anywhere."
"Oh! Peggy, how could you do such a thing?"
"There he is."
"Where?"
"There behind the door."
"Quick, catch him, or he'll run away and die."
"Oh! Peggy, how could you do such a thing?"
"Poor, poor Billy, poor pussems, poor cat."
"Heavens! Whatever shall we do to get it off?"
(Scream) "... Be careful, you'll stick it in his eye."
"No I won't."
"Yes you will."
"No I won't."
"Give him to me, I know what to do."
"No you don't."

"Yes I do."

"No you don't ... she's painted her dress too, look! It's green all down the front."

"Oh! Peggy, how could you DO such a thing?"

"You can't paint cats, they don't like it."

"Look ... here's something that will take it off."

"No it won't."

"Yes it will."

"What about his ears?"

"Leave them alone."

"His fur?"

"Don't touch it."

"She's got it on her hair, too."

"Oh no!"

"Oh yes!"

"Oh no!"

"OH! PEGGY, HOW COULD YOU DO SUCH A THING?"

And so on. By this time I was in a hopeless muddle about everything. But one thing I knew for certain, my first painting was not a success, and that awful feeling of being in disgrace in front of a lot of people, whose disapproval I did not understand, was a most uncomfortable experience.

It was Hester who saved the cat. "Don't worry, dear," she had said later, "Billy never suffered from any cause of the paint because I cleaned it off." The cat survived, and lived for many more years.

Shortly after that my mother decided it was time I went to school. I felt apprehensive, waiting, fearing that beyond my area of safety a frightening world was moving nearer.

My first day at school was a jumble of confused impressions which alarmed me. When my mother knocked on the school door my heart began to hammer, which must have been noticeable, as at that age I was all skin and bone, and wore long tight-fitting jerseys. The teacher who opened the door pointed at my thudding heart and said—to my horror, "Goodness, what is wrong with her, she looks terrified." I felt acutely ashamed as well as scared, and as nothing was done to lessen my fear, it increased, and this in turn seemed to affect my sight, as I could not see anything very clearly.

When my mother had left me, I found myself surrounded by noise, confusion, disorder, brick walls, wooden benches, banging doors and grown-ups, looking like giants, shouting incomprehensible things over mountains of children all pushing, squirming, shoving and bumping into each other. When the tumult had died down I was made to sit at a long table and given a slate on which I was expected to write down strange marks called figures, and do something with them, called Arithmetic. I got hopelessly lost, and never succeeded in understanding this subject. In fact I was unable to concentrate on anything owing to the fact that I was in a continual state of tension wondering what was going to happen next.

Punishments for making mistakes or for misbehaving were variable; they usually consisted of standing in a corner of the room wearing a dunce's cap, or standing on a stool facing the class. Being sent outside in the corridor was just as bad, as one was likely to meet the Head of the school, Mrs. Kipp, a rather short, stout, leather-bound looking woman dressed from top to toe in black cloth, who gazed at one through pince-nez, and shouted like the Red Queen, "Come to my room when the bell goes," where one would get a long and severe lecture "for one's own good".

"Disgusting . . . I won't have it in my school—vain," Mrs. Kipp said to me one day, in front of the whole class. "You must have them removed immediately." She was pointing at the silver snake bracelets that my mother had put on my wrists when I was one year old. I was bewildered. I felt as if I had been born in them, and had forgotten they were there. When I got home, I could not understand my mother taking so long to decide what to do, and I was disappointed when she finally took them off. "I will keep them for you," she said. But I had a sense of loss, and it took me some time before I stopped going about feeling strange, and undressed.

Some of the children were worse off than I was, being feeble-bodied, and sometimes scolded for it. One round-shouldered child was forced to wear a back-board, which they said would keep her back straight; anyone who even slouched had the same treatment. Wetting one's knickers, which some of the children did regularly, was a dreadful disgrace. The offender was isolated and made to sit in a corner; and bullying was frequent.

During break or between lessons or outside the school gates, things were just as bad. I tried to keep my eyes down, and run home before I found myself in the midst of raging, tearing, furious fights, that were almost ceaseless as soon as the teacher's back was turned; often I would emerge from a pile of scratching, kicking bodies and run panting to the refuge of the oak trees, where the silence was blissful, and I would wish we could learn something instead of having to fight all the time.

This school was called "The Oaks", and at the beginning and end of term we had to sing a song which started with the words:

> Oh the oak and the ash and the bonny elm tree
> But the sturdy oak is the best of the three
> We know it because we are oaks you see.
> HURRAH for the oaks, HURRAH for the oaks.

I did not feel a bit like an oak. I was on the small side for my age and, according to my brother, looked like four twigs tied in the middle. I was sorry for "The Sensitive Plant", a poem my father was very fond of reading, and I sank slowly but surely to the bottom of the class.

I do not remember having any art lessons at this time, but we must have done some handwork, as I was walking home one day holding a little paper house still wet with water-colours when suddenly it was squashed flat between the hands of a boy running past laughing. The shock this gave me was not so much due to the destruction of something created, but to the discovery that there were people in the world who enjoyed destruction for its own sake. I realised from then on that anything one valued would have to be hidden if it was to be kept safe; for the first time I knew what pockets were for and why we had so many of them. I felt safe at home, but as I was unable to express my fears I was often moody and morose.

My mother bought me some paper, and a box of crayons, and my brother Derek drew a square with some woolly marks coming out of another little square standing on the top, and I had my first lesson on how to draw a house; from that moment I could see what shapes could do. Squares could make houses, and windows, and castles, and doors, and boxes, and tables, and towers. Circles could make wheels and ponds and oranges. Straight lines could make stick people. It was not difficult to proceed to other more complicated shapes; and before long I was drawing. "A Ship in a Storm." "A House on Fire." "Gnomes by Moonlight." "My Mother out for a Walk." Very soon I found myself drawing all the time; my favourite pictures were sad and mostly to do with death. I did one of a dog dying in the snow on its master's grave—I had heard that dogs were inclined to do this; a slave dying of over-work in the cotton fields—inspired by a poem that someone had read to me. And a picture of a very old man and woman who had just buried their little dead baby in the garden. I called this "The Effects of War", a title I borrowed. My mother thought these pictures were morbid, but my father said, "Good heavens! it looks as if Ugly Pugly is going to become an artist." Niña said, "Wonderful. But not very original. However if she gives up drawing dying dogs, and works for years and years, who knows, she might get the Prix de Rome." Whatever that was. But I was happier now that I had found something that I enjoyed doing.

Running Wild

The situation at school improved. The kindergarten mistress left and was replaced by someone else. I was only aware of the change when one morning a soft woman leant towards me with a basket of beads, and told me I could make a necklace.

From that moment I was totally absorbed in a new life, even the room looked different, with the french-doors wide open so that the ivy blew in; and beans sprouted in jam-jars on the window-sill. The long benches were always covered with pots of paint, raffia, bricks, beads, glue, scissors, balls of wool and plasticine.

Sometimes the soft woman would read us a story. I liked the one about little Jesus who worked in his father's carpentry shop; and the one about Moses who was found in the bulrushes. One day she told us how the world started, called "In The Beginning", which we were allowed to illustrate. I made the sea and mountains and earth and everything growing on it, including animals; rabbits, a robin, some ducks, a giraffe, and lots of other things. My teacher gave me full marks; and all the children crowded round to see the sun I had made in the middle of the picture which had lines radiating from it like the petals of my yellow flower.

The Angry Woman

The houses at the bottom of the street where we lived were tall and narrow and semi-detached, with glass-roofed verandahs outside the first floor rooms. The front gardens were small, and ours was full of evergreen shrubs, mostly laurel and holly. The iron gate in the wall squealed slightly when you opened it, and there were stone steps leading up to the front door which was green and had a brass knocker. In the street stood a row of lime-trees which filled the drawing-room with a cool watery shade. There was a continuous shuffle in the leaves of the limes, but the stiff mottled laurel bushes hardly stirred. The shadows on the earth under the bushes were cold and dark, and nothing seemed to move there except gnats. Sometimes a cat would walk past our house rather disdainfully or scrape a hole and squat over it with a distant look.

There was very little traffic in the road, and the sounds were variable. The swish swash of the road-sweeper's broom, the tick-tocking footsteps of a passer-by, the clanging of the Board-school bell at the end of the next road, the snuffle of a steam-train standing at the railway station, the grunting satisfying munch of a cart-horse eating from a nose-bag, with a wagon full of vegetables behind him. Above all, the cries of the vegetable man and other sellers and buyers of various goods who travelled round the town, each with their own peculiar cry, which went something like IYEEE—OHA —AGAN OWANS. A harsh yodelling yell, that sounded like a lunatic with a hoarse throat, and could mean anything from "Any old rags and bones" to "Any old iron".

At the top of the hill things were slightly different. There were fewer trees, and the houses were smaller, tidier, cleaner, more modern and, to my mind, more ordinary. The front gardens were the same size, but instead of having brick walls and palings, they had well-cut privet hedges, wooden gates and rows of military-looking flowers made to grow in straight lines. One of these houses was occupied by a woman who did not like children. Whether this was true or false I do not know but, as fearful rumours circulated round her, we would walk past the gate as quickly as we could. Once we felt safe, we would roar with laughter, push each other about making hideous faces and invent dreadful jokes. Sometimes we would draw huge heads with big noses and stick-out ears on a wall with a piece of chalk. Another dodge for relieving the feelings was to blow through a privet leaf, or a blade of grass, and make a long rasping sound as loud as a brass trumpet. Whatever I had heard about "The Angry Woman", as she was called, I had certainly never set eyes on her until one particular afternoon.

The day in question must have been round about the end of July. I and my friend, Gina, were walking up the hill on our way to school. The day was hot and, feeling rather languid and slow, we stopped outside the gate and looked at the Angry Woman's house.

In spite of the heat the windows were shut and partly concealed by a garden full of overgrown shrubs and trees. There was an untidy path leading to the front door which had a dark round pane of glass in the top panel. By the side of the path I could see a few clumps of border flowers looking ragged and small.

Gina nudged me.

"That's her."

"Who?" I said.

She tried to pull me away.

"Don't let her see you."

"Where?"

"Hidden."

"I can't see her."

"Somewhere inside."

"Nowhere about."

"She'll kill you."

"Why?"

"She hates us."

The Angry Woman

"What for?"
"Remember Dorothy?"
"Who?"
 I couldn't remember anything. The scent from some kind of plant was intoxicating. Then suddenly my eyes fell on a most beautiful flower that shone beside the path like a small red sun.
 "I want that flower," I said. My hand was on the gate.
 "What, you mad?" said Gina. "Come on, let's go."
 "It won't be missed."
 "You're dotty. Hurry!"
 "Nobody minds."
 "Daft, quick I'm off."
 "She can't see me."
 "Bats."
 "Just a flower."
 "She'll catch you."
 "She doesn't care."
 "All right, I dare you!"
 Silence.
 "You wouldn't dare?"
 Silence.
 "Would you?"
 Silence.
 "Well, go on."
 The decision was taken. Feeling calm and free I opened the gate and, walking easily up the path, I picked it. It throbbed in my hand like a robin. I held it gently like a piece of glass and life seemed suddenly vivid and important. The scent rocked in my head as I walked down the path and the whole of summer swarmed towards me.
 "Run," Gina said, "she's seen us."
 One look at the window paralysed me. The flower trembled in my hand as if it had a heart. I must have dropped it then as I was shutting the gate, which I was always told to do to keep out trespassers. The woman

Running Wild

behind the window had a wide white face, with a large black hole in it that kept opening and shutting soundlessly, when suddenly the window burst open and a scream poured out like a rocket. I was off down the road with Gina, panting, frightened, half blind with panic.

We tumbled into Gina's house which was a little further down the road, and shut the door. Gina's mother stood in the shadows wiping her hands on her apron as she listened to our breathless explanations. When someone knocked on the door with a harsh insistent bang she pushed me, for some reason, into the pantry and locked the door. "Don't come out or speak," she said, "I'll see what I can do." "Say she's not here," said Gina to her mother as she followed her into the hall.

Alone in the dark I could hear voices at the door getting louder and louder, then I heard some footsteps coming down the corridor, and Gina's mother opened the door.

"Peggy," she said, "you'll have to come out. I can't do anything for you, they've got a policeman."

I was lost.

"He only wants to take your name."

The Angry Woman

Lost.

"... address."

Lost.

There was no wall to hide behind, no shield. I had even forgotten what I had done. I was taken out, right out for everyone to see. A large crowd seemed to have gathered at the gate. I heard a constant buzzing noise, and a huge black policeman filled the sky. Behind him I heard a woman screaming, "That's her, lock her up, she oughtn't to be allowed, little beast ... a lot of dirty kids ... gives the road a bad name ... nothing but a guttersnipe." I was a criminal, a thief, but almost everyone else seemed to look at me unaccusingly and curiously, as if I were in a zoo.

The policeman asked me my name. I had no name. I was nameless, and suddenly to my disgust I burst into agonies of terror and shock. Rivers poured from my eyes and nose. Tears stuck to my ears and wet the front of my dress. No one offered me a handkerchief and when my nose started running I felt indecent and ashamed. The policeman asked me where I lived. I tried to remember.

"... oughtn't to be allowed, ought to be locked up."

The woman went on screaming, and people drifted away. It was at this juncture that the policeman, who had been writing in his notebook, tucked it away in his pocket and winked at me. But it was far too late. The world had collapsed. It had split open from end to end. The world was black and I was full of shame. I wondered what was coming

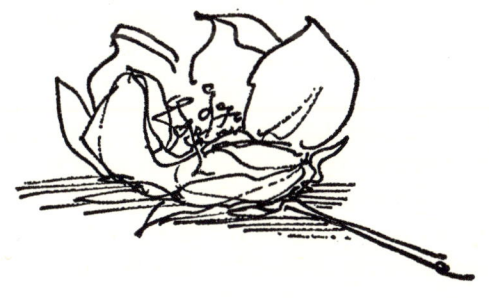

next. Everyone faded away at that point, except the policeman. He took my hand. "Come," he said, "I'll take you home," and we walked down the hill together. I was still crying and could not answer his questions.

"Too many people in the world.
"Do you want a toffee?
"You won't do it again, will you?
"Have you done this before?
"Whatever it was you did?
"What did you do?
"Take flowers without asking?
"Mustn't have that, must we?
"Is your dad at home?
"Your mum?
"Not too strict, eh?
"Have a toffee?
"Is this where you live?
"Here then?
"Or here?
"Further on?
"Well I never.
"I'll go now.
"Don't do it again, will you?
"That's right.
"Don't forget?"

He stopped just before he reached our house, and gratefully I watched him walk away. Grateful not for fear of punishment, but for being left alone. I imagine that my mother would have been impatient at my stupidity for taking a flower from "a woman without brains", and for not knocking at the door and asking for it. No doubt my father would have lectured me irrelevantly on the fact that all flowers belonged to God, and if anyone was silly enough to think they owned them, they deserved what they got. Whatever they might have said or done was unimportant. I was grateful to the policeman for dropping the matter.

The Angry Woman

The event had stretched my emotions to the limit and I was aching to forget.

It is certainly true that I forgot everything from the time the policeman left me, until the next incident, which may have happened at the end of the same day, or at the end of the same week.

It was the last day of the summer term and I remember sitting on a bench in the gymnasium watching a play being performed by the older girls. I had no idea what the play was called, but I sat giggling and fidgeting with my whispering friends. Through the rows of heads in front of me I could see a girl on the stage, floating about in a long white dress tied round the waist with a silver ribbon. She was speaking in a sing-song kind of voice. I could not see what she was doing as we were sitting at the back of the room. Perhaps the kindergarten children had only been allowed in at the last minute. Anyway, we were young and restless, continually nudging each other, shuffling our feet and muttering.

"What's she doing?"
"Being soppy."
"That's Prue."
"Who?"
"Prue—Prune."
"Ugh! Horrible."
"Look! She's dancing."
"No, she's not."
"What then?"
"She's picking up pins."
"Picking what?"
"Her ..." There was a lot of giggling.
"ssh! I said rose."
"No, you didn't."

A big girl sitting in front turned round and glared at us.

"Stop making that noise at once," she said, "or you'll get turned out."

We stopped immediately, sitting very straight in our chairs; but the voices started again.

"She's picking flowers."

"Oh!"

"If she bends too far you'll see her ..."

"Hush!"

"... bottom of her dress is all pins, it wasn't ready in time."

"Goodness! What will happen when she's caught?"

"You'll see."

"STOP TALKING YOU TWO AT THE BACK," said someone else in the front row.

"Two at the back," said the girl sitting next to me, giving me a push and going off into fits of giggles.

"And two in the front," said another girl, rolling about in her chair.

"Listen," said the girl who had scolded us the first time, "if you don't keep quiet right now, I'll go this very minute and tell Mrs. Kipp."

We were silent at once, like a row of little frogs with shocked, bulging eyes.

After a time, curiosity got the better of me, I stood up so that I could see over the heads of the audience. I saw the girl they called Prue who had just stooped down to pick up one of the flowers that were strewn all over the floor when, to my amazement, there was a long loud rumbling sound that developed into a stupendous roar, and an incredible figure dressed in gold suddenly soared through the air in a flash of light. With a shock of pleasure I recognised her at once. It was the girl with red hair. The girl who had found me one terrible afternoon standing in the middle of the classroom surrounded by paralysed pupils and a ferocious kindergarten mistress. The girl who, having had permission to enter the room, had strolled over to the cupboard to get some books and, on the way, had whispered the answer to the problem to me, setting me free of the teacher's rage.

The Angry Woman

"That's Hay Dees," said the girl at my side.

"Hay who?" I said.

"Hay Dees, the god of the underworld. You know? He comes to take poor Sefunny away; they had it this year in class; it's Greek." I did not know anything about poor Sefunny or Greek, but for some reason I was intensely excited and full of an enormous pride, as if I had been given a bag of gold. Hay Dees who was really my friend had leapt through the air like an air-borne king for lucky soppy flower-picking Prue.

I imagine I must have been too dazed to notice the rest of the play. But I skipped and hopped all the way home when I was not jumping up to catch the leaves on the trees or swinging my satchel round in a circle. I danced past

Running Wild

the Angry Woman's house as if it was a house that had been empty for some time, and had no further interest for me. I also ran the last part of the way—I was good at running—with the vision of a laughing red-haired girl flying in the wind beside me.

"What a mad thing you are," said my mother, when I got home, "whatever has happened to you?"

But I could not really explain. The effect of both experiences that week had been totally new.

The Wedding

It was nearly always summer when I was a child, when it was not Christmas or Easter, and my marriage certainly took place during that season. I remember the yellow ruffles on the laburnum trees, and the warm air smelt of lilac.

I met Tommy in the school playground during the eleven o'clock break. Our friendship lasted for three years, until his parents took him away from his aunt's house, where he had been living while they were abroad. We must have got married somewhere in the middle of that time.

The morning we met I had just started another term at the kindergarten, and was proceeding in the direction of the swings, when I saw a new boy leaning against one of the posts. He was looking thoughtfully at the other children who were eating buns, or biscuits, or bananas, or sponge-fingers, or liquorice all-sorts, or something or other and, as I noticed he had nothing to eat, I approached him and offered him an apple. He took it without saying anything, and while he ate it I studied him closely. I noticed that he was slender and fair and serious, that he had a pale gold-coloured face, and the greyish-blue jersey he wore made him look misty. He ate a little less than half the apple, then he handed it back to me and I finished the rest of it and threw away the core.

When the apple was eaten any kind of shyness we may have had seemed to vanish, and we talked to each other as if there had never been a time when we had not met. To my surprise, Tommy produced a large round sweet from his pocket, which after continual sucking, changed colour. Sucking it in turn, we watched the colours change, and the sweet grow smaller and smaller until we had got to the centre and found a tiny aniseed ball which Tommy, very generously, allowed me to eat.

From that day on we were hardly ever apart, either I was having tea at Tommy's house, or he was having tea at

Running Wild

mine. Those days, for me, were warm and predictable. After school we would run about in meadows full of long grass, where we burrowed or played at "Homes". We paddled in the stream with jam-jars, looking for tadpoles, watching the brown water-weed curl round our toes, and when the grass was cut we buried ourselves in the hay, which smelt hot, and stuck in our hair and shoes. We were considered too young to be given pocket-money, so we gathered sticks or bunches of wild flowers and tried to sell them to the bowler-hatted men who came rushing out of the station carrying black umbrellas. Usually they would rush past us, but sometimes we would get a penny, which went a long way in those days. You could get a toffee-apple for a halfpenny, and a barley-sugar stick for a farthing.

One afternoon Tommy's sisters, who were a little older than he was, told him that our marriage was to take place that very day, and there would be no more say or discussion about the matter. Tommy was sent out to fetch me at once, not that either of us had any objection; we knew that they had been preparing for it all that morning.

When I got to their house, I was taken immediately to his sisters' bedroom to be got ready.

The Wedding

"You must not see the bridegroom until he is dressed for the wedding," they said, "and he must not see you." Then some friends of the sisters took Tommy away. I stood looking in the mirror while they twisted and pulled me about and fussed. I wanted to dress myself, because I knew what looked good on me and right, but I was not allowed.

"Stop!" they said, "we are the bridesmaids. Everything has to be done by us." So they took hold of bits of material of different lengths and colours, and they pinned and wrapped them round me, so that I looked like nothing but a patchwork scarecrow all covered in rags, while they gathered about me squealing and chattering, hanging long necklaces of bright beads made of glass and china round my neck, and contradicting each other about the way they should do my hair. Worst of all they hung two bunches of artificial grapes at each side of my head, on a band, where they clacked and rattled, and I was so wrapped up I could hardly move.

When I was taken downstairs I felt sick with shame. They had dressed Tommy like a prince, in black velvet, with a long white ostrich feather curling in his cap. We had to walk together right up the middle of the drawing-room, where there was a writing-table with a candlestick on it. One very small child started to cry, because she wanted to play with the horse-on-wheels that was to take us to the honeymoon; then the dog had to be turned out, because it got too excited, leaping and licking everyone, and knocking me down when they told us to kneel on a cushion; while someone called Peter said in a very loud voice: "I NOW PRONOUNCE YOU MAN AND WIFE," and wrote our names down in an old exercise book.

"It's all over now, you can go if you want to," he said, and I was glad because I was allowed to pull off the wedding clothes and jump about again in my own dress, with my legs free and nothing on my hair.

Tommy's aunt came in then with a white cloth, which she

spread over a large round table, and she put a plate of biscuits and a jug on it.

"This is the wedding breakfast," she said. I was so thirsty I could not stop drinking. I asked her what made it so good, as I had never tasted anything like it before. But everyone was talking at once, and all I could hear was "... honey ... just water ... apple slices ... treacle ... have one ... and a little more ... ginger." I tried to make this drink at home, but I must have got the recipe wrong, as it never tasted the same.

When I had drunk enough of it, I was all for getting off my chair and going to play in the fields. But Tommy pulled me back saying, "We've got to have the honeymoon next and go to the bridal suite." He took me into a corner of the room and told me that it was in the cellar, and his sisters had spent all morning getting it ready.

"Please pretend to like it, Peggy," he said, "otherwise they will be so disappointed." I felt cold and cross and at the mercy of them all.

When they opened the door of the cellar in the back garden, I shivered all over. It was cold and damp and full of shadows. Near the wall was a spring bed without a mattress, which they had covered with an old curtain and a faded cushion. On the other side was a chair with three legs and a table with a stoneware jam-jar on it. In the jar were some dandelions, and there was a chipped plate, "in case," they said, "we wanted to eat something." And a cup without a handle, "in case we felt like having a drink." On one wall they had pasted some pictures taken from a comic called *Bubbles*. On another wall was a photograph of the King and Queen holding a baby. All over the cement floor were sheets of brown paper with patterns on them done in coloured chalk. There was a tea-caddy with a picture of camels and palm trees on it, and "Wedding Present" had been written on a piece of paper and stuck on the lid. Inside this tin was a pencil, some old cigarette cards and a

The Wedding

sheet of paper folded up. When we unfolded it, there was a drawing of a house and two people standing by it. The people were bigger than the house. Then they closed the door and it was very dark. There was a cold damp smell coming from the floor, and all the coal was stacked at the end, and I wanted to go home.

Tommy and I sat very stiff and quiet on the edge of the bed, but I could hardly bear the intolerable feeling of restlessness and I longed to leap through the door into the light again, where I could see it shining very brightly through the slit. I looked round the walls uneasily, until I saw a large spider sitting in a corner of the room on the ceiling. I clutched Tommy's arm and pointed at it. We watched the spider stretch its thin front legs in an uncertain way and walk slowly and cautiously with a slight wobble across the ceiling towards us; eventually it came up against a bumpy crack and, in trying to make a detour round it, failed and fell with a plop on the brown paper and scuttled under the bed. Tommy and I stood up at once.

"I just can't stay here another minute," I said, so we opened the door and went to look for his sisters.

"What did you think of it?" they said.

"It's a beautiful place," said Tommy.

"Yes, beautiful," I said.

"Thank you. Thank you very much," we said. We said "Thank you" so many times, they got bored, and wanted to play another game. But we had had enough of them.

"The only thing we can do now," said Tommy, "is to run away."

Tommy went to the kitchen and borrowed an old blunt knife. He also took some matches, when his aunt was not looking, and a few potatoes. He wrapped all these in a big handkerchief, which he tied at the end of a stick, and carried over his shoulder. He asked me what I had got, and I said, "two farthings", which I had been saving for a white mouse. So we set off up the hill.

Running Wild

When we reached the little wood at the side of the road, we were able to get off the pavement and walk through the bracken. I noticed that it did not smell of good clean earth any more, not since they had started putting up all the new houses. It smelt of rusty cans, and burnt-out cigarettes. Tommy said that a dead baby had been found there once, wrapped in newspaper, but it had happened a long time ago, and he didn't know if it was true. I told him that a man had been seen roaming about there, with his trouser buttons undone, and that he came running out in the street sometimes in front of everybody. This was true, because I had seen this man looking round a tree, with a dead white face and pitch black eyes that glared at us without blinking or moving. It was awful. Like looking at a head without a body. We had run away faster than I could ever tell you, but the policeman had come and taken him away. Tommy asked if I still felt frightened, but I told him that Hester had said he was just a poor old man who couldn't help himself. All the same, I was glad when we got to the fields beside the road again.

Tommy said we would make a fire, as we were now hungry and needed to eat. I did not feel hungry, only restless and curious, so Tommy sent me off to gather sticks. Most of these I collected in the road beside the field. There were houses on the other side of the road and they looked big and important, but I never saw anyone go in or out of them. When I got back I found that Tommy had set fire to some dry grass inside a ring of stones. We put some sticks on top and a potato. It took a long time to cook, and in the end it was still rather hard, but as we hadn't got a lot of time to waste, we ate some of it, as Tommy said we might not get anything more to eat for a very long time.

Then we sat and talked about getting out into the world, which seemed to be somewhere on the other side of the field. I asked Tommy what he thought the world was like, and he said that it was much better than this, with hills and valleys

and mountains and forests and deserts and jungles and sea and islands.

"And one day, when we're grown up," he said, "we'll go and live on one of the islands, and we'll do just what we like every single day."

I thought about this for a while, and then I thought about our town, with all the different shops and the grand houses, and the Coliseum with the green dome; the cinema that looked like a palace; the grey church where Hester saw angels; and my dancing school behind the sweet shop which had a deliciously shiny floor. Then I thought about the slum full of long narrow streets with buildings made of dark and dirty brick. And public houses that had loud rooms with fighting voices bursting through the doors, where men shouted at the sky, and women swayed behind them singing, and swinging bottles. Then I thought about the recreation ground which was like a great flat desert of grass with a path all round it, and a concrete square with swings and a see-saw and a slide, where there were one or two straight little trees with wire cages round them, and benches where old people sat and looked at nothing.

When I had finished thinking about all this, I had a funny kind of feeling. I felt that I loved my town and I never wanted to leave it, and I did not know how to tell Tommy or put it into words, so I got up instead, and started to stamp on the ground, hitting the grass with a stick, and yelling, "YA! YA! HA! HA! HA!" and dancing round the burnt-out fire, and Tommy leapt up in the air, whirling and shouting, and stabbing the air with his knife.

So we made a great dance to show that we were not frightened of anything in the whole world, and nobody like us had ever lived before, and I called myself Red-flower-that-never-burns-in-the-fire, and Tommy called himself Big-Bill-the-bull-who-roars-on-the-hill, and we went on dancing and dancing until we were too hot, and hadn't got any breath left, and fell on the ground panting and laughing and fall-

The Wedding

ing over each other and tearing up handfuls of grass. Then we noticed that the sun had gone out, and the clock in the church was striking four, so we decided it was time to go home.

When I got home, I had my tea and went upstairs to the top landing and searched through a trunk of fancy-dress clothes until I found what I wanted. It was a long white silk blouse which fell to my feet in folds. Round my waist I tied a scarlet satin sash and I tucked an artificial rose inside it; then I put a white chiffon scarf over my head, which made me feel like a ghost, and it clung to my nose and felt stuffy. I painted my face with a lipstick that I found in my sister's room, and I went down to the drawing-room.

When my brother saw me he rolled on the floor laughing, saying "Look at Ugly-Pugly in Mummy's old blouse!" And he tweaked the rose out of my sash and flung it in the air. My other brother caught it, and they both ran out of the room fighting for it. My mother said, "Hush!" and went on with her sewing. My sister, who was grown up and had a wild-flower face with enormous eyes, said, "She puts us all in the shade, but the horrid little beast has been using my lipstick." I went and sat on the floor by my mother, who put down her sewing, and took the chiffon scarf off my head and stroked my hair.

"When I was your age I used to dress up too," my mother said, "but it was my brother, your Uncle Rory, who was the wild one in our family, no one could do anything with him, he even refused to go to school. Rose, Charles and Maggie were all dare-devils, but Rory was the worst. They put him on a boat bound for England, but before anyone could stop him, he had jumped overboard and swum ashore. I was the only one who knew that he spent most of the time roaming the island with the coloured boys getting into scrapes. For all that he was my favourite brother, generous, warm-hearted and always kind ... slept most of the time with a gun under his pillow ... No dear, that was later, when he was grown-up, as I said, when you were not listening; they put him in charge. He was the only one they respected and liked. If there was any trouble brewing, he was usually in the middle of it. Once there was a terrible fight, and his best friend was killed, no, I don't know how it happened, but just before he died he made Rory promise to marry his sister which wasn't a very difficult promise to keep as they had always loved each other.

"Sometimes I had adventures too," said my mother. "I used to escape to Port of Spain with Fly. It was unheard of for young girls like us to be seen in the street without a chaperone; so we used to wait until everyone was resting, and then we'd silently slip out of the back of the house. If we saw anyone who might have recognised us, my friend shouted FLY!—that's how she got her nickname. She'd take my hand and we'd run like mad, which was not very easy in long skirts and petticoats. The men were so prudish. I was scolded once by a certain gentleman.

"'Mary, my dear,' he said, 'I fear your skirt has hitched itself up a little bit at the back, and I can see your ankles. I hope you don't mind me mentioning it, but it looks so unladylike.'

"'Why, Mr. Wilkinson, don't you like my legs?' I said, as I lifted my skirt up as far as my knees. The poor man went crimson. Such impertinence; but the whole island was like that—so small, no one had anything to talk about. When I met your father at a dance," my mother said, "his ship had docked at Port of Spain. Everyone was shocked because I didn't wear a tight-waisted dress. I designed and made a Grecian gown, which swirled all round me like the waves. Your father noticed me and we were introduced. Before the dance, I had rubbed my face with flour to try to cover the freckles. They were as big as plates, I was always being told. When your father proposed to me I said, 'But what about my freckles?' He was so surprised. 'What freckles?' he said.... I think that's why I married him."

The Wedding

"Did you want to go out into the world?" I said.

"I always wanted to come to England and see snow falling, and live in a little village, and hear the bells ringing."

"I would like to live on a tropical island like you did, with mangoes and bananas in the garden, and swim in the sea, and suck sugar-cane all day."

My mother smiled. "Most of the time it was much too hot. There were centipedes in the garden, and sometimes a scorpion. In the sea there were jelly-fish that stung. Anyway, it is not the place you live in that matters, it's the person you live with."

"I like living here with you and Hester and Tommy," I said. But I knew that some time I would have to go out into the grown-up world, which I found strange and disturbing. My mother started singing a West Indian song:

> If you like-ahs me,
> And I like-ahs you,
> And we like-ahs both the same,
> Two live as one,
> One live as two,
> Under the bamboo tree.

That's all I can remember of my wedding day. The glass doors opening on to the verandah, where one could hear the shuffle of the lime leaves, and the shadows in the drawing-room mottled and waving like water. My mother's hands cool on my head, and feeling sleepy and satisfied. The world coming closer, but not too near, as my mother was singing.

In the Dark

At night the house was too dark, too tall, and had too many shadows. The worst time was after I had been put to bed. Lying alone I could hear the slightest sound. At that age my hearing was so acute I could have heard a feather falling—even the furniture seemed to threaten me then. There were always exceptions, like my mother's dressing-table, where in the day-time I could find cowrie shell necklaces, eau-de-Cologne and handkerchiefs smelling of the cuscus grass sachets in which they were wrapped. A little drawer at the top was filled with pearl buttons, brooches, violet cachous and one or two old halfpennies. One could always find a halfpenny or a farthing somewhere in the house, at the bottom of a cupboard, a bowl, a work-basket, inside old vases or tins. Then there was the double wardrobe, a vast plump mahogany object, with drawers all down the middle stuffed with clothes, satisfying in the day-time, but alarming at night when it was inclined to come alive and creak protestingly like an old lady in boned corsets. Another two-faced piece of furniture was the tall sideboard in the dining-room, which looked in the dark like a black oak chapel, with gargoyle faces grinning and growling on the cupboard doors. When someone turned on the light, they changed into ivy leaves. I liked touching it then as it was knobbly and gnarled, with unexpected bumps that became acorns instead of noses.

The safety of such objects, which I needed to balance the shadow world of ghosts, depended on the light in which they were seen; although some corners were inviolate like the deep wicker chair beside the stove in the kitchen, which was always full of comics, and cats turning round and round to get comfortable.

During the day when the house had no shadows, when the dust hung in the air like gold after the corners had been swept, and the canary sang to the sewing machine played by my mother, my house was a safe house. But at night I felt enclosed and the dark rolled in, leaving me only a small space in which to move, while everything outside was grave and dangerous. I never really understood the dark. My mother thought that she was protecting me by trying to shut it out, but there must have been another door, forgotten, or overlooked, through which I received some knowledge of its presence.

My father was dangerously ill, that much I knew, which was odd because I seemed to see him everywhere, walking up and down, up and down. I sat in the kitchen where a bell was constantly ringing, hearing exclamations, sighs, odd words, questions which floated towards me leaving permanent marks.

"He's spent most of the day going round the house locking all the doors ..."

"... and the windows."

"The doctor said he'd have him locked up if ..."

"Cruel, I thought."

"... said it was overwork ... and he fainted twice."

"She'll see him through, she's got the makings ..."

"Poor kiddies."

"Last night he never went to sleep, sitting there all night with a gun saying, if Mr. Johnson came, he'd kill him ... Whoever heard of a Mr. Johnson? ... there's the bell now."

Always bells ringing, demanding, restless, peremptory bells. Later, days later, the fuss had gone out of the air, but not the disembodied sentences.

"He just lies there now all the time, doing nothing, nothing. Talking, talking."

"Talking of it all, she never slept ..."

"I'll take her up a cup of tea."

"... everyone must take a turn, it's as much as anyone can do."

One day the bells stopped ringing, and I remember seeing my mother again. "Your father's had 'flu," she said, "you can go up and see him now."

In the Dark

Everything looked the same, except that there was a fire in the grate in the big bedroom where my parents were sitting. My father was up and dressed and sitting on the edge of the bed smoking, laughing, and talking, talking. A restless, fussy, fidgety atmosphere surrounded him, and soon I was bored and uncomfortable and left the room and forgot about it all. I was told much later that he had broken down from overwork with no one to help him through it except my mother.

The night was always the worst. It was not that I could put my fears into any tangible shape. My mother left the gaslight burning slightly, but the room was depressingly dim and the gas kept popping in the mantle. There were creaks on the stairs, in the landing and in the other room. I was afraid of burglars and I covered my head with a blanket and pretended to be asleep. When the fear became intolerable I called for a glass of water, my cat, another blanket, the cat had gone down, another glass of water and once, as an experiment, "There's a noise in the corner"—silence as we both listened—"I can't hear a noise, now try to go to sleep." So I had to call again later for another glass of water. I lost the art of falling asleep quickly until my mother went to bed.

Some unnameable thing seemed to be connected with the dark; and any calamitous event that happened in the neighbourhood, even if I was only on the fringe of it, affected me with despondency and dread. Perhaps my family felt the same way, as the meagre information I was given about such events removed them to a distance where they became mysterious and frightening.

There was the case of Skinny Lizzy—the nickname we gave her—who, according to Hester, "had become unhinged". We would watch her through the kitchen window as she shambled up the street, walking as if her bones made her feel uncomfortable. Occasionally she would stop and point at something that no one else could see, and once I saw her scolding a bird sitting on a twig, shouting at it,

63

Running Wild

with her flat hat bobbing; but usually she hurried along the road looking at her boots and arguing with them. Mrs. Lipton, Skinny Lizzy's mother, was much harder to forget, not that I ever thought about her much, until early one morning I woke from a nightmare dream to the sound of an explosion of breaking glass. I waited, listening, but the room was silent and cold; the frost seemed to be getting through the window, so I covered my head and as nothing else happened I must have fallen asleep again.

Voices were hushed and uneasy as I went down to breakfast, and everyone walked away from me except Hester who handed me a bowl of porridge.

"It was the milkman's cart, wasn't it?" I said, imagining all the glass and puddles in the road. "I suppose it fell over."

In the Dark

"It was worse than that," said Hester, "it was poor Mrs. Lipton; she fell out of the top floor window right through the glass verandah to the ground below. The milkman found her lying there all cut about but still breathing, so they took her to the hospital; not that she'll live, poor soul; she won't want to live, with her daughter being what she is, and no one to take care of either of them. 'Depressed' your mother said, but how she climbed out of that little window, Peggy, we shall never know: we shall never know that, dear, never." From then on I could not think of Mrs. Lipton without seeing a picture of her lying on the black ground, surrounded by broken glass, alone, and no one going to help.

These pictures merged with others of the same distressing character. A woman who came to the door for bread ... a dog dying ... a boy run over by a car ... and a broken-legged horse; there they lay at the back of my mind, helpless, frightened and waiting for attention.

The top half of the house felt alarmingly far from the bottom of it, and I was drawn to an attic landing window, almost at floor level, which was easy to step over. Outside there was a parapet without a rail, with a steep drop on three sides. I would stand on it trying not to imagine what it was like to fall, wondering if I could climb the ladder to the roof. When my mother discovered me there, she nailed up the window, relieving me of the compulsion to test myself in this way.

Another less disagreeable occupation was to hide between the chest and the old hat-stand in the hall, where I was completely concealed by coats. I would pretend I was invisible, while I observed the comings and goings of my family, hoping perhaps, by these means, to become part of the grown-up world where I so often felt excluded.

Just as summer seemed to last for ever, so winter never seemed to pass. It was a time when the trees dripped cold drops, and I found it uncomfortable to play outside in the garden, where the ground was soggy with black leaves. It was appallingly gloomy to see rows and rows of houses behind a constant mist of rain. I went for walks along the grey streets that looked hard and harsh, where stunted trees poked out of wire cages like skeletons, and rain-drops fell from the branches making rings in the puddles, which were full of the reflections of clouds and lamp-posts upside-down. I walked through them as if I was entering another world, sloshing my wellington boots with water to make them look like black glass.

My mother, having a special sort of grace, could look beautiful in any season. Wearing a fur coat as thick and as soft as a tabby cat, and her silver hair coiled at the back of her head, she walked down the road singing:

> Let the rain come pitter patter, pitter patter down
> In that little old English town,
> But we never mind the weather
> When we always walk together
> In that little old English town.

And her velvet eyes were warm as she said, "I've forgotten most of the words." But so light-hearted did she seem that I skipped along beside her feeling gay, and the sun nearly came out then and there, and the buds almost burst into leaf.

Spring came and went, and summer arrived and there were invitations for picnics and outings. On one occasion I was invited out by the parents of a friend for a drive in the country. They had a brand-new car, but the main thing that I remember about that day was the man we met in the road.

We had got lost, not that anyone minded. It was an occasion for gaiety, with ginger-pop drinks and apple-pie. The sun was so hot it was stifling, but we were cool inside the car and we sang silly songs, played Riddle-me-ree and

In the Dark

made a lot of noise. The car lumbered up and down the dusty lanes as Eva's father searched for the right road. We found it in the end, but it was just as lonely, apart from one man walking down the middle carrying a case. There were no paths at the side of the road, only trees and rough grass and hedges.

The man turned round when he saw the car coming and made a signal to us to stop. I did not hear what he said to Eva's father as the engine was running, but I shrank away from him as I thought he looked ugly. There were lines round his eyes which made them look strange, like the eyes of some kind of bird that can only see in the dark, and his skin was dull and pasty. Even his clothes looked wrong, his coat was too small for him and his wrists and hands were white. What I found most distasteful was the shabby sickness of him, and I was relieved when Eva's father drove away suddenly, as I had just seen him look at us in a cold, unfriendly way.

"What did he want?" said Eva.

Eva's mother was fanning herself with an imaginary fan. "The lunatic asylum," she said.

"WHAT?" said Eva.

"Yes," said Eva's mother, "he wanted us to hurry about it too. 'Up the road,' he said. I ask you. Why, we haven't seen a house in miles."

"What did you say to him?" said Eva.

"I said we were too full up. Well, we are, aren't we? What with all those egg sandwiches," she chuckled.

"You can't be too careful," said Eva's father.

"We're too full up," said Eva, rubbing her tummy. We both rolled on the back seat laughing.

"If he had got in," said Eva's mother, "I would have got out."

We found this even funnier. The man had no more effect on me and I admired Eva's father for being able to handle the matter.

One of the nicest things about summer was going to bed in the daylight. I used to stand at my mother's dressing-table while she put my hair in curlers, made of strips of paper or rags, telling her about all the things that had happened to me during the day, particularly anything that was funny, as I liked to see her smile. I saved my story about the mad man for the end, watching her face in the mirror, waiting for her laughter, but there was none.

"Don't you see, Mummy?" I said, "we were too full up. Too full up with what we'd eaten, don't you see?" My voice faded away at the sight of her distress.

"Do you mean to tell me, Peggy," she said, "that they couldn't give that poor old man a lift? A car with plenty of room, only two small children sitting in the back?"

"He wanted the lunatic asylum," I said, wondering what had gone wrong and trying to put my mother on the right track.

"Yes," said my mother, "he wanted the lunatic asylum, and they hadn't got the decency to give him a lift. Only one small case he was carrying you said, but they hadn't any room. Only at the end of the road he told them, but they hadn't got time."

"Why do you think he wanted it?" I said. I was feeling disappointed and a little angry. I had made my mother unhappy, when all I wanted to do was to make her smile.

"Think," she said. "Imagine—perhaps his wife was dying, and the hospital had called him; not everyone has a car. Or maybe, he has a little girl who is very ill there, and she was asking for him. Say he wanted to see someone he loved?" By this time I was beginning to experience a feeling that was new, so I did not recognise it.

"Or perhaps," continued my mother, "he was the one who was ill, and hadn't got the strength to walk down the road. Well, anyway," she added, as she tucked me up in bed, "I must say it doesn't surprise me. I never thought those people had any imagination."

In the Dark

When my mother had left me, I lay for a long time thinking about what had happened. I was annoyed at first, not having pleased her. I had made her look flushed and shocked with a deep kind of sorrow for "that man" and then, suddenly, everything changed. I was glad, glad that she had shown pity, been angry, spoken up, and I admired her, and my friends dwindled to the size of dwarfs, and their words were bad words, and the man stood alone, and I saw him just as if he was standing directly in front of me, and this time I could see him quite clearly.

A pale, tired, worried-looking man, instead of the ugly one I had imagined. I felt sure now that it was short-sightedness that made him peer at us so closely. I remembered that he had not seemed at all resentful when he had been refused a lift, just resigned, as if he did not expect to be helped; patient, perhaps, or hopeless; a bit on the small side and rather thin, and now I was really seeing him he definitely looked ill. At that point I was overwhelmed, as my mother had been, with compassion and indignation. The only way I could release myself from such a sudden emotion was to dream a wide-awake dream.

To Eva's parents' amazement I had taken charge of the situation, insisting on the man being given a lift. I imagined myself stepping out of the car in an imperious way and saying, "Unless you give this gentleman a lift I shall refuse to get back in the car." As it was a dream, naturally my instructions were obeyed and the end was a happy one, with the man arriving at the hospital in the nick of time to be reunited with the one he loved.

I found myself having to dream this dream over and over again before I was satisfied that I had done all I could for the man, who if I ever think about him is still walking, waiting to be helped.

My fear of the dark seemed to cease gradually after this time, particularly as I had learnt to read, and my mother got worried as she was afraid I would ruin my eyes. I was

Running Wild

getting older too, and I began to identify the shapes I saw in the dark. One had only to touch them or look closely to discover that they were familiar bits of furniture. Sometimes they were personal belongings which one had not recognised, and their shadows were often distorted in a bad light. Not that fear ever ended, as far as I was concerned; it simply shifted from one region to another. One moved about with what light one had.

The Trap

At the bottom of the garden I had dug a small square hole for my tadpoles and was lining it with clay hoping it would dry hard in the sun and hold water, when I heard someone puffing on the other side of the fence and I saw Georgie's red face looking down at me through the leaves.

"Whatcher doin'?" he said with interest. So I told him.

"Cor!" he said, "not bad. I think I'll do the same."

I despised copy-cats, but held my tongue as I needed companionship.

"'Ow do yer make it?" he said. When I started to show him, his interest flagged.

"Lot a work fer nuffin'," he said. "I'm catchin' butterflies over 'ere."

"Where?" I said, trying to see down the path.

"Beauties. Better 'n frogs. Why don't yer cum over? My mum wooden mind."

"I'll go and ask my mother," I said.

I found my mother pacing about the drawing-room searching for scissors. She often looked like a person making her way towards a place far away from home: perhaps that was why she was always dropping or losing things—handkerchiefs, thimbles, spectacles, gloves, a brooch, a book, or a packet of needles; she would call vaguely for my assistance, and I would follow behind her, handing them back, or discovering whatever she had lost underneath a cushion, or in some unlikely place like the toe of a shoe. Her eyes were often sad, but she had a slight wry smile as if she found life amusing, if not quite to her taste.

"Georgie?" she said. "Oh, Peggy, I wish it didn't have to be him. If you're not careful," she added irrelevantly, "you'll end up by marrying an errand boy."

"I'm not going to marry anyone," I said, "I'm just going to look at Georgie's butterflies."

"Always running about the streets with goodness knows who. You'll never be a lady."

"So can I go?" I said.

"That house has never been the same since the Viners left," she continued vaguely. "Pass me the cotton, there's a dear, I must finish Niña's dress tonight, she wants to wear it tomorrow, and don't be long."

I sped round the front of the house to the one the Viners had vacated, and found Georgie in the back garden beside the herbaceous border. It was very hot as there were no trees or shrubs to give it shade, but the flowers were brilliant and buzzing loudly with bees. On the path there were several jam-jars turned upside-down with a few cabbage butterflies fluttering and flopping about inside, and one or two Peacocks; but all the cushions of purple blossom on the bed, I noticed, were covered in Red Admirals and Painted Ladies.

"What are you going to do with them, Georgie?" I asked. "Have you got a butterfly house?"

"A what?" he said.

"You know? The kind with a glass front."

Georgie looked blank and frowned. Bending down he

The Trap

put his hand under one of the jars and drew out a white butterfly by one of its wings.

"See," he said, "that's a good'un, isn't it?"

The butterfly was flapping violently like a bit of paper in a strong wind. I was just going to tell him to hold it in a different way when, to my horror, he tore off one of its wings and then tearing off the other one, dropped the wriggling body on the ground. After gazing at it with curiosity, he lifted up his foot and stamped on it.

"See," he said, as if he had done something important, "'s easy. Nuffin' to it really." Frowning with concentration, he picked up an empty jam-jar and handed it to me.

"'s not difficul'," he said, "look, I'll show yer. Jus' put a jar over one like that, see?"

At that moment a window above us opened suddenly and a woman looked out.

"Georgie, your mum wants you."

Georgie hurriedly pushed the jam-jar in my hands. "I won't be long. Honest!" he said. "See 'ow many yer kin catch."

I was left standing on the path holding a hot jam-jar in my hands, and thinking fast. I felt emotionally confused: concerned for the butterflies, angry and disgusted with Georgie, and underneath it all realising that I could not be rude to him in his own home—as I had so often been told; and I felt a kind of shame for my hatred of killing things, and having Georgie find it out. Most of all I wanted to go home. I walked down the path and, tipping each jam-jar over with my foot, I watched as all the butterflies fluttered away. When Georgie came hurrying down the path again I waved an empty jam-jar about in an ineffectual manner.

"I'm sorry, Georgie," I said untruthfully, "I stumbled over your jam-jars and knocked them down, and I can't catch a butterfly. I've tried and it's much too difficult." I waited for Georgie to tear off my wings and tramp on me, but he just looked bored and indifferent.

" 's all right," he said, 'you couldn 'elp it, we kin always catch sum maw, can't we?"

"I've got to go now," I said, "I thought I heard my mother calling me."

"My mum," said Georgie, "wants me to go to the shops." I started to walk away.

"You'll cum again won't yer?" he said.

I opened the squeaking gate and ran back to my house. Furtively, and rather shamefully, I looked through the hedge to see if Georgie was still killing butterflies, wondering what I would do if he was, but to my relief the garden was empty, the front of the house as blank as Georgie's face, and in spite of the heat the windows were dark and tightly shut.

That same afternoon my father, who always went for a long walk in the country on Saturday, brought home a live rabbit. He had found it caught by its leg in a trap. I came out of the house to find my family standing round this rabbit like some people gather round a road accident. The rabbit's leg was mashed and bloody, and it lay without moving, its eyes wide open. No one said anything, except my father, who appeared to have brought back the rabbit as evidence to prove that there were people living in the world not fit to be called humans, monsters who let dumb creatures die slow and horrible deaths by inhuman methods. He enlarged on the horrors of such traps, waving his arms about as if giving a lecture.

No one seemed to be doing anything for the rabbit. My mother said there was nothing anyone could do. She went to get some brandy, and brandy and milk was put into its mouth with a teaspoon. Very shortly after that it died. I cannot remember it being dead. I can only remember the rabbit's eyes, shocked and terrified. I wished that I had known a few little rabbit words to comfort it. When it was dead the problem was solved, and I wandered off feeling bored; bored with the helplessness of adults and their inability to act. Death did not frighten me. I had been told by

The Trap

my father, who I believed in such matters, that death was just another adventure. It was the cruelty, the violence that needed to be confronted.

It was arranged that we would return the following day to the place where my father had found the trap, and remove it. Sunday was as warm as Saturday. Cucumber sandwiches, bananas and hard-boiled eggs were put into a basket with a bottle of lemonade, and we caught a train to Pinner Woods.

We never found the rabbit trap, and everything looked beautiful and good. I had never seen so much country in one place. When my ears had got adjusted to the silence after the diddley-dum diddley-dee of the train rattling away into the distance, I discovered that the air was full of little sounds which mounted, if one was listening carefully, to a musical roar. This was so intoxicating and inviting that it had the effect of making me want to run everywhere at once.

"That child gets quite hysterical when she's in the country," said my mother.

I ran away from the sound of their voices and the sight of slow-moving people wearing too many clothes. The grass almost reached the top of my head and was swinging and singing. The hot tufty ground ticked like a clock with insects and the flowers hummed continuously. A soft dust of gnats revolved round any tall plant, and bumble-bees shooting through the air bumped into me, sizzled with surprise and grumbled off indignantly. I raced through the grass picking buttercups as I ran, following a path up the side of a hill, until I came to a wood where the sounds stopped suddenly and I found myself walking on flat ground. Tall ferns rose in the air and curled over my head like feathers.

I stopped and looked at the trees which were even more exciting, particularly one, which was shorter than the others and easy to climb having plenty of branches. I got to the top and felt as if I could stay there for hours. I lay in the crotch of the tree as in a nest, and felt at home and at ease with everything—almost as if I had some power, understanding the language of animals, and could, if I came to be trusted, be in possession of their secrets.

I don't know how long I was there, but it was when I wanted to get down that I found I was not alone. A man was standing underneath the tree unaware of my existence. The soft ground must have deadened the sound of his footsteps, as I had not heard him coming. I crouched further down in the tree and tried to breathe without making any noise, hoping I was well hidden by clusters of leaves and twigs. After what seemed hours, I looked cautiously through the branches at the man who was now leaning against the tree and peering from side to side, as if he was hoping not to be seen. I was beginning to get frightened, until something else happened which alarmed me more. Along the path came a herd of goats, big ones, with twigs and tufts of grass sticking to their shaggy hair. Although they moved slowly and quietly towards my tree, their horns looked sharp and curled threateningly. The man started to back away from them, caught his coat on a spiked twig, which he extricated with some difficulty, and rushed off down the path. The goats, snuffling noisily, congregated round the base of the tree and stood there comfortably, as if they had no intention of ever going away.

I was glad the man had gone, but I did not want to get down. In fact I knew I could never get down while the goats were standing there looking at me. "Why don't they move?" I thought, "why don't they go away? Why have they picked on my tree?" The magic had suddenly gone, I was just a very small human being dependent on other human beings bigger and more powerful than myself.

There was a scrunch of leaves and, to my relief, I saw my father walking through the trees towards me. I called him, and when he looked up I started talking rather foolishly, praising the distant views, which I pretended I could see from the top of the tree, and telling him how

wonderful everything looked. My father asked me why I didn't get down.

"The goats," I said pointing at them as if I had only just seen them. My father waved them away with his walking-stick. The goats heaved off, their heads nodding as they trotted into the shadows where they stopped and watched us curiously. I climbed down the tree.

"We've been looking for you for a long time, we wondered where you'd gone. We've got to hurry now," said my father, who was always hurrying.

On the way down the hill I told my father about the goats and the man under the tree.

"You're a Capricorn all right," he said.

"What's that?" I said.

"A sign of the Zodiac. Half goat, half fish—it's the sign you were born under. I expect the goats recognised you and came to protect you."

I did not know what he was talking about, but for some reason I felt a whole lot better.

At the bottom of the slope I saw my family. They were all sitting in the long grass and munching sandwiches. From a distance they looked just like the goats.

The Village

We spent our summer holidays on the north coast of France, in a little fishing village that lay between the hills on top of a cliff. Most of the cottages belonged to the fishermen who were lean and strong. They sailed fat black boats with brown sails, and they got drunk on Saturday nights. In the morning one would see a few of them lying like old hulks in the rough grass, or even in the street. Once I saw a man sleeping it out on a pile of little stones near the road, snoring softly on a Sunday, when the bells were ringing in the little church behind the bushes.

They were a hard-working people, fierce and raw, and their houses blazed in the hot sun. They seemed to need colour as a child needs sweets. Whitewash and tar first, then strong bold paints. Terra-cotta or blue, blood-orange, apricot, olive or pink; sometimes one whole wall would be tangerine with slate-blue stripes round the windows and shutters. The doors in summer were nearly always open, and the front rooms looked tidy and neat, with well-scrubbed pans and cooking pots and a big double-bed covered in crochet and lace, with high white pillows. Usually the bed was in a cupboard in the wall. When a man got too old to fish he would upturn his big-bellied boat and cut out a door and some windows and live inside it; then he would grow vegetables, and have a goat to keep down the grass, and gulls would sit on the roof.

We stayed at the Hotel de la Crevasse. There were only two hotels in the village and ours was the best, or so I thought. The other one was right down the slope of the hill where the beach was flat and empty. The sand-dunes there seemed endless; they rolled into the distance giving me a feeling of desolation. There was an invisible boundary on this beach, which I never crossed alone without a sense of uneasiness. The place seemed to hum with loneliness and I would race back to the slope of the hill that led to the village again.

Running Wild

Down the street I would watch the women as they went to the water-pump, carrying buckets hanging from yokes on their shoulders. They wore long petticoats, with their skirts and aprons furled round their waists or humped in panniers. Sometimes they wound a small black shawl round their heads to keep their hair from blowing about; unless it was Sunday, when they wore a bonnet with a starched frill that framed their faces like a huge fan. Every day when it was not raining, they would tie up their skirts and clamber down the cliff with baskets on their backs and fill them with sand, which they brought back and sprinkled on the floors of their houses: this, I was told, was to keep them clean. In the morning, the old sand would be swept into the streets to be replaced with fresh. They would smile and shout when they saw me, then laugh and talk excitedly together when I did not understand.

I enjoyed wandering about the village alone, amongst the ducks and geese and chickens that paddled and pecked in the thin stream that wriggled like an eel through the creamy dust at the side of the road. Most of the water came from the overflowing buckets at the pump, or from the slops emptied out-of-doors. The road was clean for all that. In those days I had a strong sense of smell, and I knew. I remember every single scent in that street, whether it came from seaweed or thyme, hot bread or clover, wet sand or wine, incense or soup, dry grass or coffee, and always the smell of good or bad weather everywhere.

The hotel was very rarely full, as at that time, rough country villages were not considered to be the most comfortable places to spend a holiday, and often we were the only English people staying there.

My mother and father drank coffee and liqueurs with Madame at the wooden table in the saloon bar where sand was sprinkled all over the floor. The sitting-room was stuffy and small. It had an upright piano, and orange wallpaper decorated with large black roses and leaves. The hotel had

The Village

only two floors and all the long windows had shutters.

Every time new visitors arrived, I would run to the window, hoping to see someone of my age to play with, but usually they were old or invalids, and none of them stayed very long. Some of the guests were strange, like the woman in dark glasses, wearing strings of beads and a long feather-boa, who wandered up and downstairs as if she was waiting for someone; whoever it was never arrived, and she left the same day in a taxi.

I used to follow Lizette, with her mops and beeswax polish, as she made the corridors shine like glass. Lizette had a hump on her back, and a sharp face. She talked constantly to me in French; but as we did not understand each other's language, we usually ended waving our arms about in mock anger, making rude and exclamatory noises, trying to shout each other down with considerable enjoyment. Madame would then appear and put a stop to it and take me down to the kitchen where Marie-Louise, who was soft and kind, would let me taste the crême-de-chocolat.

I was glad when my mother had an invitation to tea from "the ladies who lived on the hill". There for the first time I met Riki. By then Tommy had gone out of my life, having been taken away by his parents, and I never saw him again.

I met Riki sitting by himself in the long grass. He smiled at me and I sat down next to him, and we tried to communicate with each other. He could not speak English when I first met him, but he taught me a verse that I repeated after him, and can remember to this day.

> Un petit bonhomme
> Assis sur une pomme
> La pomme de gringole
> Comme ça vole.

By various signs he managed to express his desire to have a friend, and I hastily assured him that I understood and

needed one too; after that we knew at once that we belonged to each other, and I felt excited and secure. We promised, by more signs, that we would see each other as often as we could.

The dark boy, as I called him, had black hair that fitted like a fur cap, his eyes were huge and brown, and he called me Pegee.

Riki and his cousin Dinah were looked after by "the ladies", their great-aunts, while their parents were abroad. They lived in a house called "Chalet des Mouettes", a thick stout stone building with an overhanging roof, which stood on top of a hill looking down on the village. To get there you had to climb up a narrow sandy path, between boulders and gorse bushes, until you got to the top where the wind roared, slapping your face and making your hair stand up on end. The Chalet stood firmly in a sea of wild rough grass that tossed all round the walls and over the stone steps that led to the front door. The door opened into a large hall with a flagstone floor and a flight of stairs which led to an upper

The Village

gallery where one could look over the banisters into the hall below. The doors in the gallery passage opened into the bedrooms.

There were three sisters living in this house. Auntie Prissie who looked after the children, Auntie Milly who supervised the servants and did some of the cooking, and Auntie Laura, the Theosophist, who believed in fairies and saw auras; sometimes people would nudge each other and chuckle and whisper about "Auntie Laura's auras". But I liked Aunt Laura best, and I was most impressed when she told me she possessed a photograph of a real fairy. There was always some reason why she could not show it to us, "Not now dear, I'm too busy." But we were never in doubt that it was genuine, and in a way it made her one of us. None of these sisters had married and they had looked after their brother's children, and their brother's children's children, while their parents were abroad.

Riki and his cousin were the last on the list to be cared for at this time, but Riki was not very happy. Auntie Prissie loved Dinah, his little cousin who had green eyes and clover honey hair, but Riki was dark; Riki might be no good; Riki might not be anything. Riki came to me without being able to speak a word of English and tried to tell me all about it. I could not understand a word of French, but I sensed what he was trying to say, and this drew us closer together. I often wished that he had his mother with him. I had only seen her once, but she had given me the impression of being a completely white sort of person, in pale silk, with a skirt making a sound like see-she's-fleecy-too as she moved about, and drop ear-rings tinkling under her whipped cream-coloured hair. Riki took after his father, who was square and solid and strong.

My mother told me that Riki's grandmother was a princess, but this information was unimportant to me at that time, and I forgot all about it.

Riki and his cousin knew many other children—John,

Running Wild

Stephanie, Natasha, Gwen, Philip, Bennie. As we were never under the eyes of our parents, who had their own interests, we roamed about together all day. I now felt like a member of a community, and the beach belonged to us. The sands were vast; the sea went so far out it seemed to disappear into the sky. Even when one reached it there were lines of little waves in shallow water stretching right out, until one got to the rollers that were sometimes blood-red and emerald green with seaweed.

At high tide on a windy day, the sea roared and hissed and sucked its jaws between the rocks and leapt into the air sending up great spouts which exploded in spray or sheets of water that descended without warning from unexpected places, leaving our hair dangling like wet snakes. Bennie could manage the sea at the top of the tide. He was much smaller than any of us and thinner, but he knew when and where to swim and how. He would slip into the water and the waves would lift him up and over them until he reached another rock, and they would wash him on to it. He would swim from rock to rock until he was so far out, we could not tell if he was a bird or a boy. When he found one he liked, he would lie there looking like a seal and dreaming. John and Philip could swim amongst the rocks when the sea was rough, but they made a lot of noise about it—splashing, gasping and shivering as if they had been for miles, when all of us could see that they had just been in and out. Most of the little ones, which included myself, stayed behind on the rocks dancing about in the spray.

At the bottom of the cliff was a small natural platform of grass, with a rock on it like a table, where all our families assembled. Very few people visited the beach and our pitch was reserved early, but if anyone dared to use "Our Rock" we gathered in rows like baboons and stared them out of it. On the top of the cliff was a footpath to the village that passed through a field full of boulders and bushes, and trees twisted by the wind.

Running Wild

Sometimes, if I was on my own, I would leave the hotel and go up the cobbled street in the opposite direction to the beach, past the pump where the women clattered their pails of water, until I reached a path winding up a hill on the left. On the top of this hill was a stone house belonging to a sculptor called Monsieur Gil; he had been known to scoop the clay under the rocks on the beach to model the heads of the fisherpeople. Sometimes he carved them in a sea-green coloured stone.

It was a small hill but so high that the little stone house seemed to be rushing past the rolling clouds and turning round the world. It made me feel giddy; I wanted to sweep the clouds away from the dark blue sky and stop everything from moving. Then Kiki the goat would come and bleat and nudge me affectionately, and Monsieur Gil would open the big double doors and let me in.

In sign language and a few French words I tried to explain to Monsieur Gil that I wanted to be an artist too, and I was proud when he asked me which of his pictures I liked best. I pointed at a drawing of an old woman with a shawl round her head, telling her beads under the light of a lamp. It was done in pencil on a dull orange-coloured paper. Monsieur looked pleased, and I felt that I had made a good choice.

The studio seemed full of people in stone or bronze or clay. It looked as if the whole village had got into the room. There was a drawing of an old fisherman and his wife walking on the shore with baskets on their backs, which had been drawn as if they had grown together like two old stones. There was one of a girl in a fan bonnet standing on the quay in the fish-market. There were pictures of houses and boats and the sea. The whole place seemed to smell of salt-water and fish. The sculptured heads of the old men smiled and were quiet, and the women looked as if they would stand there for ever and ever. It seemed as if the sea had given them a secret which they shared in silence. Once the secret

The Village

had been understood, they could look the sea in the face and stand on their own ground. Monsieur Gil did not have to go to sea to receive his share—he discovered their wisdom through his hands. The big stone heads were heavy and grand with their own knowledge, and his understanding of it was there in his sculpture for everyone to see.

It was often while I was having thoughts like this that Monsieur Gil would have a visitor—usually a girl from the village, holding something in a napkin, a cake perhaps or some loaves. His mood would change. He would suddenly lose interest in me, and taking me by the arm, he would put me out on the steps and shut the door. There I sat feeling bewildered and bored while Kiki came and nosed in my pockets looking for chocolate.

After a time Riki and Dinah and all of them would sweep up the hill looking for me.

"Pegee, Pegee, come along, what are you doing there?"

I would tell them what had happened.

"Moomoo said that she wouldn't be surprised if more than one girl didn't visit him," said one of the older children. I thought I knew what that meant, but I was not sure.

"They all visit him," said Gwen, who was young and inclined to exaggerate. "He's so poor, if they didn't feed him he would starve to death."

"That's just gossip," said Natasha reprovingly, "my mother said that every bachelor needs a housekeeper."

Riki put his arm round me. "Poor Monsieur Gil," he said, "I don't suppose he has anyone to love him like we have," which made me feel better, and we were soon racing down to the shore again.

I used to return to the hotel tired out with running about all day on the sand. I have no clear memories of the village after dark, when everything in my drowsy mind seemed to float and merge together. The fishermen came back from Boulogne after a day's catch or a week's fishing and often went dancing with their girls in the hall near the hotel.

Monsieur Gil once lifted me on the window-ledge to look at them, but the noise was deafening, and the couples swirled and stamped without any grace. After the crashing of waves I preferred to listen to the warm silence which was full of delicate sounds, like the fiddle-playing wind in the telegraph wire, and the crickets in the dry grass.

In the bar of the hotel the bottles on the shelf reflected all the lights, and faces swam towards me smiling. The floor was gritty with sand, and there was shouting and laughing. The bell over the glass door would ring through the evening and bottles and glasses clinked and tinkled. My mother sat at a table with a serene face, talking to my father or Madame who sometimes got up to serve a customer. I was given milk with a bar of chocolate to break up and melt in it and a roll fresh from the baker's oven across the road. There were large pans full of thick whipped cream for the coffee, which was ladled generously.

The billiard room was in action with balls clicking and voices raised in encouragement. Someone played the piano in the other room. Through the window the night looked green with black figures moving up the road, while lighthouse beams swished across the sky. When I was in bed I could watch the signal from two lighthouses playing on the walls. The nearest one swept round the room three times; then there was a pause and another one, much further away, filled the room with a soft pale glow and gradually faded out. This had a soothing effect on me. I felt like a baby being rocked in a cradle of light.

Quicksands

The day came when my family sailed back to England leaving me at the Chalet with Riki and his cousin and their three aunts. I was now in the care of Auntie Prissie who gave us our lessons. In addition I was to be taught French, which was the reason why I was left in France, but I do not remember learning very much except new forms of loneliness. The Chalet became a different place as soon as my parents had gone. The village was out of bounds unless we were accompanied, and we could not use the sitting-room which was the only comfortable room in the house. The wind was either sighing or moaning round the house, or roaring and whipping up the grass and banging on the shutters. I felt imprisoned, without knowing why, in an atmosphere that was distant and cold. Auntie Prissie sent me several times to a room at the top of the house as a mild punishment for inattention, but chiefly because she thought I could work better without distraction. I only remember the empty blank face of the room, the windows rattling in the wind and the rain outside sweeping by like a mist. It was worse than being handcuffed; a pain in my left side crept into my arm and I rocked backwards and forwards trying not to cry for home. I was used to a family life that was warm, intimate, disorganised and overcrowded. The Aunts gave me a taste of winter and their rules were incomprehensible to me.

I slept in a large room with five empty beds in it. The swishing reflection from the lighthouses gave me no comfort now, and I spent long nights aching for my mother and the comfort of home. The interior of the Chalet was wood and there were earwigs everywhere which frightened me as I had been told that they settled in one's ears. Daddy-long-legs sizzled on the walls and got caught in my hair; even tiny insects were magnified in my imagination and I spent long senseless unsuccessful hours trying to catch them and put them out of the window. In time I became resigned to occasional bouts of depression which I could not express to anyone, not even to my mother as my letters to her were read by Auntie Prissie before they were posted and had to be formal.

Auntie Prissie had a quiet manner and a voice hardly louder than a whisper, but she made me afraid. I sensed an undercurrent of disapproval in her that could come to the surface at any moment and sweep us under her wrath.

Auntie Millie ruled the kitchen and kept hens. She was as tough as a sorbo ball, with a temper as unpredictable as a thunderstorm. I was often woken in the morning by her screams of rage as she scolded the peasant girls who came to work for her in the house. I hid my head under the bedclothes and stuffed my fingers in my ears, but it was no use, nothing shut out the thunderous roars of reproof.

Apart from the inevitable Scotch porridge, the food was good: I have never tasted better, particularly the bread which was home-baked. It was the colour of old ale and had holes in it big enough to see through. We used to have what was called a goûter: thick slabs of bread and banana and French chocolate which we ate while playing in the grass. For some reason Auntie Millie left me alone, but she sometimes got angry with poor Riki—on one occasion forcing large lumps of cold porridge down his throat which he could not eat. Such a humiliating scene made us both suffer. But her rages came in cycles. Once they had worn themselves out we could expect a lull for a week or two.

In spite of the food, I was skeleton thin, and as Auntie Millie never scolded me, she may have identified me with one of her cats, of which she had a vast number. We forgave her much for roaming the moor and bringing home the kitten abandoned there, often tied to a bush and left to starve. A child rarely interested her, but a cat was a different matter, particularly an ill-treated one. She was a contradictory uncomfortable character and we took good care to keep out of her way.

Auntie Laura was always in the background, passive and

pale, moving about like a little white-haired mouse. I often wished that she had the care of us, but she was always in Boulogne giving English lessons, or wrapped up in the spirit world connected with Theosophy.

Auntie Prissie was concerned for the people in the village, and baskets of food were taken to the elderly who were visited from time to time. On one such occasion, in early winter, we walked to Hardelot, which was about three miles away, to enable Auntie Prissie to take food and other necessities to a crippled old woman. Auntie Prissie herself was by no means young; her hair was white and she had the sharp parchment-coloured face of an old lady. To get to Hardelot, which was a small village built on the sand, we had to walk along the beach where there wasn't a sight of a house or a human being or even a seagull, and the sandhills hummed with that peculiar lonely sound I usually only seemed to notice when I was alone.

We set off to Hardelot one November afternoon when the air was cool enough to keep the village people indoors. Auntie Prissie, as straight as a winter tree, walked with her black cloak swinging from side to side, and no hat on her white hair. Our legs were bare as we did not feel the cold, and we ran about in front or lagged behind Auntie Prissie, who carried a basket of food covered with a napkin. On the way we passed a bull that lunged at us behind a low wall made of big stones, and we were worried to see that there were gaps in it covered inadequately with briar and nettles. The bull stamped along the field keeping pace beside us, snorting and making a hard sound with his hooves, as if he was tugging up the grass and banging it down again, all the time breathing with contempt and blowing warm steam through his nose and puffing. Auntie Prissie walked forward silently at the same pace.

"Don't take any notice," she said, "I'm sure he can't get out." Riki caught me by the arm and whispered, "What would you do if the bull escaped, Pegee?"

"I'd run, of course. Wouldn't you?" I said.

"I couldn't. Pegee, don't you see? Auntie Prissie's too old to run. I'd have to stay with her."

At that I was terrified. I knew I could never leave Riki and it meant we would all have to die for someone who did not seem to care for us or anyway, not for me. The conflict between staying and running was still pulling at my mind, when the bull came to the end of his field and bellowed until we were out of earshot. I was relieved to be out of danger and full of admiration for Riki's loyalty and courage.

To buoy up our belief in Auntie Prissie's ability to take care of us, we dragged up all the old legends about her. In the war Auntie Prissie had been walking across a lonely moor at night and a crazy soldier attacked her. Auntie Prissie had been able to defend herself, and the man had run away. When a drunk man had shut himself up in his house and refused to talk to anyone, Auntie Prissie had been able to get in, while everyone outside had tried to pull her back. The man had listened and agreed to stop ill-treating his family and never touch another drop. Auntie Prissie could sense the coming of the "Little Whirlwind" when everyone else was out-of-doors. She always closed the shutters in time and the windows were never broken.

"Auntie Prissie could do ..."

"Auntie Prissie had been ..."

"Auntie Prissie was ..."

By that time we had arrived at the beach, and were walking along the sands to Hardelot.

The sea was so far out we might have been in the middle of the desert. The sandhills on our left stretched away into the distance, looking light against the dark blue sky. We kept on chattering to fill the silent air with sound, while now and again we sank up to our ankles in little patches of flat damp sand.

"No roaming at Hardelot now," said Auntie Prissie, "there are quicksands about."

"Oh, where?" asked Riki.

"Not far from the village," said Auntie Prissie, "just keep near the houses."

We went on walking, splashing through the pools and picking up shells. Vast transparent jelly-fish had been left behind by the tide, and the sea had described its passing in the sand with a pattern of rippling lines. Little yellow crabs, no bigger than spiders, were scuttling between the ridges of the ripples.

We played "I Spy", and the chain story game.

"Once upon a time there was a little girl and a little boy, and they lived by the sea ... it's your turn now."

"In a village called Hardelot—your turn."

"One night there was a terrible storm, with thunder and lightning and rain and snow, and everybody heard a terrible cry—it's your turn, Auntie Prissie."

"Nonsense!" said Auntie Prissie.

"Go on, Riki," I said.

"It was the little boy and the little girl crying for help. They sank in the quicksands and were never seen again. One by one everybody went out to look for them, and the quicksands swallowed them all up—your turn."

"When the quicksand had swallowed up all the people, it wriggled its way to the village, and all the houses sank for ever under the sand. That's the end."

"Quicksands can't swallow houses," said Riki's cousin.

"A quicksand can swallow a whole horse and cart," said Auntie Prissie, "so you watch your step."

I watched my bare feet slapping on the sand and I felt depressed. After what seemed a terribly long time we saw Hardelot, standing like an abandoned village amongst the dunes.

To me it was like the end of the world. There was no one about and there was a shut-up guarded look about the houses. Sand flowed round the walls and over the doorsteps. There was no grass, so there were no goats. We walked barefoot up the road, feeling the cool sand slipping through our toes. There were a lot of bushes and some people had draped their washing on them to dry. Long thin ribbons of smoke rose from some of the chimneys, and an old woman with black eyes stood staring at us from a window. I felt disappointed when Auntie Prissie knocked on a cottage door and, giving us a bag out of her basket, told us to go and eat our tea on the dunes.

"But not too far," she said, "and come when I call."

I was looking forward to sitting in front of a fire, surrounded by warm walls, drinking café-au-lait.

We climbed up one of the highest sandhills from where the village looked like a heap of wrecked ships after a

Quicksands

storm. We slithered down the dunes once or twice and tried to play "Pig-in-the-middle", but the threat of quicksands coloured our games and made us afraid, so we sat at the bottom of the hill and looked at the sea and talked.

"Auntie Prissie said it was somewhere over there."

"In summer it's different, there are lots of people."

"In winter you lose your way and that's when it gets you."

"There are sand yachts in summer."

"No, they're too poor to have sand yachts, that's further on at Le Touquet. Anyway, real people live here."

"What's 'real' people?"

"People who don't just come in summer."

"Who would want to come here anyway? There ought to be a danger notice somewhere."

"If it wasn't for Auntie Prissie, poor Augustine would die."

"She looked all right when she opened the door."

"Perhaps she knows where it is, or maybe she never goes out."

"I think I remember a story about a horse sinking. They tried to rescue it, but they couldn't get the cart off, and the whole lot disappeared. The sand covered them up, and it looked all smooth again."

"How awful!"

"When a man begins to sink you can't rescue him, or you'd start sinking too."

"What happens to him?"

"His eyes pop out of his head and he suffocates, but you don't hear him screaming, because the sand gets in his mouth."

"How horrible!"

"Let's play 'Hide-and-Seek'."

Nobody moved. The sun was going down and everything seemed to have a shadow. We ate our rolls and bananas and chunks of chocolate.

"Auntie Prissie said that a woman went out collecting mussels, but she never came back."

"Perhaps she drowned."

"Or went to live in another village."

"Or ran away to sea."

There was a pause while we tried to believe what we had said.

"What happens to them when they get to the bottom?"

"They never get to the bottom. It's bottomless. You go on sinking for ever and ever. Something pulls you down and you can't stop."

"You must stop some time."

"What does it matter if you're already dead?"

"Why don't they put a fence round it?"

"They can't do that, because it moves. First it's in one place and then it's in another one."

I looked with fear at the sand dunes behind us.

"It's an awfully dead place," I said. "It's just as if everybody had gone and died."

"Once a little girl took some eggs to her grandmother; when they went to look for her, all they could find was a pair of shoes."

"That's Little Red Riding Hood!"

"No, it isn't."

"Why didn't her shoes sink then?"

"She'd taken them off to play in the sand."

"Does it take a long time to die?"

"How do I know? I've never died. Anyway, nobody knows because they go so quickly, and there isn't any mark in the sand after."

I got up. "Come on," I said, "let's play 'Touch Last'."

So we played 'Touch Last' and 'Grandmother's Footsteps' near the cottage walls; but we had no heart for it, and were glad when Auntie Prissie came down the path and gathered us about her again.

The sun was sinking into the sea as we walked back along the beach, but there were no more quicksands to frighten us. The tide was coming in, and we had to paddle across a wide stream of ice-cold water which I enjoyed, as it made me feel like a great explorer. Auntie Prissie gave us some little gingerbread cakes to eat, and we walked beside the sea and were soothed by the continuous thudding of the waves. The moon came out and everything was visible, even the stones on the beach. The sandhills looked like a mountain range, and we paddled in the creamy edge of the sea until the cold was knife-sharp and we put on our socks and sandals again. It was exciting walking in the dark with the sand-crickets jumping round our legs, and seeing the stars reflected in the pools. I was busy imagining the kind of things that might have happened and composing a letter about it to my mother:

"Darling Mummy, yesterday we went to Hardelot to see a woman who was dying. Auntie Prissie took her some food,

so she's all right now. We walked for miles and miles and I wasn't a bit tired. Riki got caught in a quicksand, but I saved him just in time. I flung him an old rope which I happened to have on me, and tugged and tugged until he came out. Auntie Prissie said that if it hadn't been for me, we should never have seen him again. We had to cross a river when we came back, otherwise we would have been cut off by the tide. The water was very cold and came up to our necks, but we got back all right. Auntie Millie says, 'All's well that ends well.' Did I tell you about the bull? It escaped into the road and nearly killed Auntie Prissie, but Riki and I didn't run away. We managed to get her into the next field, where we were all safe. Well, darling, you mustn't worry about me. Auntie Laura thinks I'm going to be a great poet, because of a poem I wrote, which I will show you when I see you. Look after Hester and tell her I shall soon be back with you all."

We arrived at the Chalet absolutely tired out. Riki cried endlessly in his sleep for his mother. I wanted to go to him, but I had to walk all round the gallery in the dark and I was afraid. Auntie Prissie came out with a candle and told Riki to stop. "Stop it! Stop shouting at once!" she said, as if he could help having nightmares. I closed my eyes trying to shut out the pitch-black room.

Early in the morning, when the sun rose, Riki came to my room where we played, or sat together in bed reading or talking. Riki had learnt to speak English, but I could not learn French from Auntie Prissie. I had picked up a little patois from the peasants and the songs that children sing, but when it came to Auntie Prissie's jingles I was no better than a parrot reciting them to amuse her friends.

"Regardez, monsieur, ma poupée, c'est ma fille savez-vous bien?" I would say in a flat voice, standing to attention in a stiff dress. It was inappropriate as I had grown out of dolls, but they smiled and nodded their heads as if I was progressing in some kind of way. Riki slept on the landing at the top of the stairs, where there was just enough room for his bed under the window, a chest-of-drawers, and a chair. A curtain hung across the opening, and Auntie Prissie's bedroom door was in the passage outside the curtain. He would jump out of bed and, leaning across the banisters of the gallery that overlooked the hall, he would call my name in a quiet voice. I would open my door on the opposite side, and we would talk softly, listening for the first sounds of morning; but it was always too early—there was nothing to be heard in the thick sleepy air; then he would patter on bare feet round the gallery, and we would have the whole of my room to play in with the door shut on the obstinate world outside which was nothing but a scold.

It was a time of warmth, of freedom from wrath, from frost in the voice, from iron hands marking books with crosses and little biting mouths nibbling cold words about people they did not love. It was morning and no one could spoil it. We flung off the night and pulled off the sheets and made ourselves a tent where we slept, died, got married, or plotted, spied and attacked the enemy, with both of us whispering as softly as possible, suppressing our laughter and carrying on generally in a crazy, sloppy, childish way, hitting each other with lumpy pillows, enjoying the morning without a thought that it would ever end.

Sometimes our talk was all about being grown-up, and then we would sing the songs our families sang as we acted out our family life together. Putting the children to bed; planting potatoes; coming home tired; cutting the bread; calling on people; dancing the foxtrot, serious and slow in our pyjamas and nightdress in someone else's imaginary house, where we had been invited for a party. This we would do, as well as pretending to be the hosts, turning the gramophone handle, shaking hands with all the guests and handing out cocktails.

Best of all I liked reading a book together in bed, with the windows open where we could hear the day beginning.

Running Wild

The steamers grunting in the distance as they sailed in and out of Boulogne, and the shrill high whoop of a ship's siren and all the seagulls sitting on the roof gawping and wheezing as they waited for the first scraps to be flung from the kitchen door. I had one good Polish fairy story about house spirits. The chief of them all was a little man called Casp who wore a magic ear-ring. No harm could happen to a house when they had a house gnome living in it. I liked the little fat people called Sofnips, who lived between the sofa cushions and hid things there, like cotton-reels and thimbles and all the other odds and ends one loses during the day. It was a battle between good and evil, as Casp was kidnapped and imprisoned in the forest. The story told how he was rescued by his friends, the house spirits, which included the timid little Sofnips, and brought back home with his magic ear-ring shining like the sun. That was a story that made us feel good and safe and when we had finished reading it we sat quiet, letting the things that had happened go on and on inside us, and Riki's eyes were huge. But then the cock would crow and Marie-Louise would sneeze coming up the path and Riki would jump up and slither round the wooden passage back to bed again, Auntie Prissie would call for the day to begin and we would get up and dress and go down to breakfast.

One ordinary day we were stopped in the middle of our lessons by Auntie Prissie saying, "There's to be no going into Peggy's room in the mornings, Riki. From now on that's got to stop." I cannot remember what I felt about this, except surprise at the usual incomprehensible rule. No reasons were given and Riki's cousin who slept in Auntie Prissie's room could give no satisfactory explanation.

"She just doesn't like it," said Dinah, who was sympathetic but not really concerned with the matter. So we accepted it as we accepted storms, rain, bruised legs, stomach-ache, nettle-stings and thorns, cold porridge, nasty medicine, the dark without a light and quicksands. We still had our goûter time, but that was short and the evenings were getting darker. So were the mornings, when we lay silently in our beds at opposite sides of the house, sinking into a black emptiness in which there was no present, only memories of what had passed and thoughts about what might be coming, which was always difficult to imagine. I felt lonely again as winter rushed forward with black clouds, cold floors, dead grass and a nasty little wind that had started to weep and whine.

Riki, who was not going home for Christmas and had more to lose than I, was at my door at half-light whispering that he could hear Auntie Prissie snoring in her sleep. Apart from being extra quiet, we found that there was nothing wrong with being together, so we played and talked and played, until the grey fear lifted; but pleasure and silliness made us laugh too loud and that put an end to it. Suddenly we heard a cough. A cupboard closed in Auntie Prissie's room and Riki, quick as a mouse, had gone and tumbled into bed, dropping his slippers which slithered on the wood, and I had the blankets over my head in a trice and was as still as a stone as I made myself die all over. I waited and waited; but I had nothing in the world to hope for, as Riki was too small for the size of the danger which I could not name and the enemy whom I did not understand. Eventually I got up and dressed and went down to the dining-room.

I was informed that Riki was not allowed up for breakfast. There was no taste in the food I was eating, and I looked at the wall and thought of nothing. Riki's cousin came up to me with her kitty-cat's eyes and said softly, "Auntie Prissie won't let Riki get up or eat anything until one of you owns up."

"Owns up to what?" I said.

"To him being in your room. If you own up she says he won't be punished."

This statement roused my distrust and increased my con-

fusion. I struggled to understand why Riki had refused to speak, but I never realised, until I was older, that "owning up" to Auntie Prissie meant owning up to doing something wrong. Riki, without realising it, was proving his integrity. Silence, to him, was preferable to the admission of a lie.

Everything looked a kind of dull white—the plates, the dishes, the jug, the milk, the spotless faces, the table-cloth— or a heavy dark grey, but that was all inside myself, like

Quicksands

fear and not knowing why anything was happening, or what anyone was going to do next. Outside the winter mist was thick, which made the windows look like the eyes of a blind man. Auntie Prissie rustled towards me and everything was black like a cell with the door slammed and her voice whispered and hissed like a cold draught.

"Did Riki go to your room this morning?"

Why did I hunch myself up like a tortoise, instead of sitting up straight and thrusting out words?

"Did Riki go to your room this morning?"

My head went down and a strand of my hair got in the milk. I held my porridge spoon in a tight grip, as if it was all I had to hold.

"Did Riki go to your room this morning?"

"Well, she wouldn't hit me," I thought, for Dinah had told me that she couldn't hit me, even if she wanted to, as I was someone else's child.

The rustling moved away, but there was no relief from conflict. If Riki had said "no" to her questions, how could I say "yes" and make him out a liar? Logically, it seemed to me, she must punish him all the more. If Riki had refused to say anything, then she was encouraging me to be a sneak. Auntie Prissie played the waiting game, until the tension was unendurable. The whole day was like hunting a fox; it was like prison; it was like nothing on earth. Luncheon came and went.

"Poor Riki," said Dinah.

The food went down my throat like stones.

"Auntie Prissie knows he went to your room," she said. "All she wants is one of you to say so."

Nothing made sense; my mind slumped to the bottom and stayed there. "How could I betray a friend," I thought, "and help anyone, least of all myself." I had nothing to guide me now; I could only wait for Riki to act. I was more silent than that awful silent day. There was a weight in my head and I felt as if I was sinking for ever and no one would ever know. Like a flash in the dark I seemed to see Riki in a coffee-coloured jersey, as I first saw him, when he sat in the yellow grass with his jet-black eyes shining, and excitement bubbled up in me and stabbed like lightning—and then it all faded as the dinner-gong rumbled to summon us for supper.

Riki's cousin came to me and whispered, "Riki has confessed and Auntie Prissie says that he has been punished enough, but no one must ever talk about it again." When Riki came into the room I looked for his misery, but there was none. He had a slice of bread and was sucking the jam off his fingers. He looked happier than Auntie Prissie, or anyway more relaxed, as if he had stuck it out to the limit of her endurance. His face had a washed clean look as if something had been accomplished.

"When we're grown up," he said, when we were alone together, "we'll never let anyone spoil things for us, will we?" I did not answer; being grown up was all too far away to imagine, and Auntie Prissie faded into the gloom of my mind, a silent dim retreating figure in black.

When I was older I understood the reason she had separated us, feeling thankful that I had not known at the time. "Little boys do not go into little girls' bedrooms, my dear." I also knew a little more about Auntie Prissie from the odd comments that passed from one grown-up to another: "... was a governess," I remember someone saying, "she adored him but, being as she was, she left that very day, and never entered the house again." "Oh poor ... but Mary dear, one has to think of the children." "Yes, of course, but they were all so fond of her, and loving him as she did, she refused to marry anyone else." After hearing this I had no doubt that Auntie Prissie had been tormented in her time, and the deprivation in her life had shaped our own.

"Priscilla is a fine woman," my mother said, "she would always do the right thing, but Peggy never learnt anything while she was there."

After the isolation of a wild winter on a hill, shut in the Chalet, home was like a mad-house, full of restless activity with people running up and downstairs, shrieking and laughing and slamming rattling doors. The overture to the Christmas season started with visits from friends and relations who left nothing in my mind but fragmentary impressions, some of them strange. Auntie Gertie had hysterics because she said that my mother was worshipping idols. My mother had been burning cones of incense inside the brass Buddha on the writing-table and rather enjoying the scent of it, when Auntie Gertie walked in unexpectedly and flung up her arms and started wailing. My mother gave her brandy and sent her to bed with a hot-water bottle. We could hear her moaning, "Oh Edrie, oh Edrie," all the way up the stairs. Edrie was my father's nickname for my mother. But Auntie Gertie was a little dotty and always arrived without warning at the wrong time, carrying a suitcase full of medicine bottles and pills and a little spirit stove to heat a kettle in the morning.

Aunt Hilda who I liked, was dotty in a different way, being inclined to histrionic behaviour and uncontrollable laughter. She had the ability to create drama out of the most unpromising material. When I met her for the first time, she had left her husband in foreign parts and had come to live with us, bringing her little daughter who was so quiet she moved like a child in a dream. This dream-like impression was accentuated by her candle-white face and hair so red, it seemed to smoulder. Aunt Hilda, on the other hand, was restless and talkative. She would follow me about the house filling my head with stories about her exotic gardens full of humming birds, and trumpet-shaped flowers blowing out bees as big as pom-poms. If I got tired, she would switch the scene to candy-coloured mountains tipped with ice, and waterfalls sky-high thundering earthwards. Mostly she was concerned with death.

Running Wild

"When you feel the earth is pulling you down," she would say, "that means you are going back to the place where your life began. When you are young you almost float, but for the old, there's a need to return to the earth and sleep. Life is a continual process of being drawn down towards the ground. I feel that happening to me now," she would continue dramatically. We would stop talking and wait. When nothing happened she would go on evoking the scenery she loved. Jungles where she had seen huge stone carvings of snarling gods standing amongst twisted trees; bells ringing on women's arms as they danced; snakes rising from the hair of men with magical powers who could see in the dark and foretell the future; black rivers pouring through snow-covered rocks where the donkeys stumbled, but tall pattern-clothed women walked smoothly carrying water-jars on their heads.

Sometimes she would describe a tragic moment in her life, such as the day when people were fighting in the streets of Lima in Peru, or the night her baby son died in her arms with convulsions for lack of proper medical help, an event which affected me deeply. Aunt Hilda was a laughing, sobbing, whispering, gasping woman walking constantly about the house looking for someone to talk to who was ready to listen.

Visitors came and left without reason. They might stay a month or an hour. Euna and her sister Muriel arrived from Orkney. Muriel moved as if there was no such thing as time, but Euna jerked and darted and asked straight blank questions and did not like being in our house alone at night.

One evening, on Hester's day off, we heard the back-door knocker bang. So, keeping close together, we walked downstairs to the basement. The gaslight burning there was so dim that the corners looked like caverns, and the passage smelt of mould, coal and old linoleum. Euna opened the door slightly then, panic-stricken, slammed it shut, shouting

Christmas

for help. I watched without being able to move, being more paralysed by the sight of her terror than any intruder. Hiding behind the coats, I saw her scuffling and pushing and leaning hard against the door which she eventually succeeded in locking and bolting with a great iron rod that looked more suitable for a castle. Euna clung to my arm as we crept up the stairs together to the main hall, while she whispered frantically about a man trying to get in. I stood in the background as she flung up the window and shouted boldly to whoever was down below to "Come out and be recognised", or some such words, and my father stepped out of the shadow into the light. "Euna," I heard him saying, "what is the matter with you, why don't you let me in?" So it all ended in hysterical laughter. Our house in winter was overwrought. One false note, however slight, would set everyone's nerves jangling.

I remember my eldest sister, Toddy, just off to a party in a blood-red dress trimmed with white fur, looking like a gypsy madonna and leaning over my bed to say good-night, enveloping me with scent and affection. My other sister, Niña, who lived at home was getting more involved, owing to the number of her boyfriends, in Father's jealousy, and forced by him to twist whatever gift she had for drawing into any field he considered financially promising. Her anger bubbled up in her adolescence and boiled over, and sometimes I found myself engulfed in her rage. I was impressed by her fury and might have been terrified, but for Hester who stood in front of me with her arms stretched out like a gate barring her way. In time I seemed to understand Niña's anger, and gradually she became no more frightening than a briar-rose covered in thorns—her arms like twigs jabbing in the air, with fingers full of brushes and paints, screaming and stamping her feet as she found her life baulked at every turn. To escape the conflict she went often to the new gaudy gold-painted cinemas, taking me with her. We used to clutch each other's arms when we got excited, and munch sweets furiously and continually while we waited in suspense for the happy end.

But, for me, the Christmas season started with my birthday and the arrival of my godmother. Every year, until she died, she took me and my mother to the theatre to see a pantomime or a play. We were swept up to London, where I was dazzled by the display of lights flicking and flashing off and on, changing the puddles in the streets into red and blue water. Inside the theatre my godmother waved us into the circle seats, where I held my breath as the curtain sighed sideways to the sound of the orchestra beating below the stage, promising delicious mysteries to come. I sat on the edge of my seat in a state of tension until the end, when the mystery was solved and there was a final burst of clapping as the actors poured onto the stage. The arrival in the interval of a tray with a silver tea-pot and cups and cucumber sandwiches was a small price to pay for being whisked into a dream world. I left the theatre in a trance, feeling enormously tired and excited as if I had been drinking something hot and fizzy with bubbles in it. I leant against my mother's fur sleeve in the roaring tube-train and fell asleep until we had to get out.

At that time we had Kathleen, from Ireland, who came to help Hester in the kitchen. Kathleen said she saw the Devil sitting at her father's table back in Ireland, County Clare, but Kathleen saw the Devil everywhere. She saw him in my toy monkey, and when I was asleep one night she burnt it, before anyone could rescue it, in the kitchen stove—not that this set her free of him, poor Kathleen. Soon after that, she left us to go to another job, but her new mistress said, "The Devil must have got in her, so many things were missing in the house, I was obliged to send her packing to another place." Poor Kathleen went off with the Devil himself in the end, or so it was said. Hester and I never knew the truth of the matter, but we often pondered about her on dark nights.

Christmas

Little Jesus was hardly born in our house. My father shuddered at the thought of a church full of best hats, and the artificial intoning of routine words while people fell dead in the streets, of starvation. He wrote articles instead of attending services and stood on platforms and spoke, and tired himself out walking in the gutter wearing sandwich-boards, while people threw rotten words at him and passed him by. My mother tried to raise money and wrote letters about the conditions to her mother in the West Indies, who replied, "My dearest Love ... he that takes the sword, shall perish by the sword ... if you are to be a martyr to any cause ..." but it was obvious that my grandmother was looking out of the window at a cornflower-blue sea and longing for nothing but the sight of my mother.

Little Jesus was too small for me to see at Christmas, but I kept him in my Bible on a glossy card which I would not have swopped for anything else, on account of the fact that someone had painted him to look like a real baby.

Christmas was unforgettable. Christmas was royal and white and dark with crackling stockings, and empty streets full of surprised bells ringing in unexpected corners. The house was hardly big enough to hold us all, and my mother carefully dug a sixpence out of the pudding and gave it to me, while everyone pretended to be surprised. Neighbours called and stepped laughing amongst the balloons to sit on chairs, while we played on the floor with our new toys, and they talked about nearly forgotten days and old times. In the evening, when the fires were dying, I went to bed to lean against some inappropriate but cherished present, like a pencil-box or a fluffy toy that turned out to be as hard as wood. My mother retired early, and Hester dragged her feet and said, "Tomorrow is another day."

It was never the same when Christmas was over, just dark and more dark and fog or rain, and everyone went back to work. Visitors left with dripping umbrellas, dashing to the station shouting, "We'll come again soon." The tension snapped suddenly, and the house collapsed into a sluggish doze.

"Look after Hester while I'm away," I said to my mother, as we were driving off in a taxi. My brother Derek took me back to France. He hated words and was nervous of everything except the sea. We were the only passengers to walk the deck of the ship, which felt like something in a fairground. Ahead of me I saw the boat soaring up to meet the sky, then diving down again while waves, foaming at the sides, heaved into the air like grey whales and rolled past the ship with a sucking slapping motion.

"Is it rough?" I asked, feeling uneasy and unsteady on my feet.

"No," said Derek, who was nervous of me, "not a bit rough, quite a nice day on the whole I should say." A reply that reassured and bewildered me, as the little channel steamer rocked up and down through the windy day.

It was dark when we arrived at the Chalet, and the shutters were banging at the windows when I was put to bed. The last sight I had of my brother was from my bedroom window the following day. Hearing the sound of footsteps swishing in the grass, I ran across the room in my nightgown to look out of the window. The wind had died down and there, in the dim mist of the morning, I saw him disappearing down the hill. Auntie Prissie had told him that there was no need to say goodbye.

The Quarrel

With the return of summer everything glistened in the sun again and the Chalet recovered its original splendour. The hall looked spacious rather than bleak. The black-and-white flagstones were satin smooth, and the bees-waxed wood shone as yellow as a tiger's eye. The seasonal swarm of visitors began to arrive, which included the Aunts' nephews and nieces and their friends, and the rooms hummed with the sound of several languages being spoken at the same time. We listened with a sharp ear to the distant roaring of ships blowing off steam as they sailed into port, which might mean the arrival of a new visitor.

The room I slept in was soon full to the brim with laughing girls. They covered the beds with scarves, bathing-wraps and flashing evening clothes; they hung silk stockings over the bedsteads, and walked about in crêpe-de-Chine camisoles with lace. After a day on the beach they tumbled on the beds undoing their hair and shaking sand out of their shoes or, standing in front of a mirror with their hands on their hips, they would appraise a new dress or an evening frock in taffeta, satin or silk, all decorated with beads or sequins, fringes or frills. Parties were arranged, and the girls were driven to a dance in the village, or to the Casino at Boulogne. They would rustle out of the house with their skirts going swiff swoof, shiff shoof, and their beads and bangles jingling and ringing, and I would listen to them laughing and talking as they disappeared down the hill into the lamp-flashing, sea-sighing night. When they returned it was late and their shuffling clothes and giggling whispers would wake me from comfortable dreams, but I felt cradled now in a crowded warmth and soon fell asleep.

The boys and their friends put up some tents in a field near the cliff where they camped and cooked, and this became a general meeting-place for all of us. There was a path across the field where the village girls carried their baskets of sand. The boys had given up trying to help them, finding the load beyond their strength. Panting and sweating, they were forced after a few steps to stop and hand the baskets back to the girls again. Laughing at their efforts, the girls would swing them on their backs with ease, carrying them with the aid of a strap round their shoulders or foreheads, then they would roll away over the grass with their skirts billowing in the wind, talking excitedly when they thought they were out of earshot.

Riki's uncles were young, with smooth dark hair and black eyes. With a hint of their mother's royal manner, and a little Scottish blood for toughness, they had a flamboyant confident charm and an intense interest in living pleasurably. Riki's aunts were as beautiful as water-lilies, unwithered by the wintry care of his great-aunts Prissie, Millie and Laura, who retired like doves in the background amongst exotic foliage.

There was Gwyneth who was small, with long ebony-coloured hair; and Bronya with her purring, husky voice, and continual laughter; and Veronica, who always dressed in beautiful sheath-like clothes and looked like a flower that must never be touched. But Tessa was the one I remember best. She was as relaxed as a bee full of honey, and could take command without being forceful. She carried a Japanese sunshade which looked as if it had been dipped in oil. Twirling it round her head like a catherine wheel, she would walk down to the sea with a sensuous grace.

The excitement roused by all this unusual activity seemed to sharpen my sight, and the world was singing with colour. The wind blew the sky clean, and the new grass flowed like water round the walls. The short trees were permanently shaped like dancing figures. At the back of the house the hens fluffed themselves out in the hot dust, and dozed under the bushes. All round the hedges and over the boulders on the hill a creeper trailed with pale green leaves and little purple flowers. Each flower was like a star

The Quarrel

and had a yellow centre; it was always covered, I noticed, with tiny silver snails. The gorse and blackberry bushes were thick and grabbed at passing skirts. We dared each other to dash through clumps of thistle and nettle, rubbing our legs with dock-leaves afterwards to relieve the stings. Sometimes we were sent to get water from the pump at the bottom of the hill, but it was hard work carrying the buckets slopping with water back up the hill again. On the beach the waves smacked on the rocks and flung up fountains of spray, while the sea boiled with creamy froth and sucked its jaws like some old cold animal, and roared and spat at us again and again. But the wind was getting warmer. The air round the Chalet was full of hot scent from the thyme-covered ground and the smell of seaweed floated enticingly across the hills.

Riki and I burrowed through the long grass to get behind the bushes where we had a hiding-place, which we called our home. Now the holiday had started we played there as often as we could. One day, when I was considering that a flat-topped boulder I had found would make a good table, Riki came towards me with a tense unhappy look on his

face and said, "Dinah has just asked me who I love best, you or her; I had to say her because she's my cousin but, as you know, I really love you best. You do understand, don't you, Pegee?" I did not say anything, but I knew I did not understand. No! Not at all! I tried to think of something to say, but nothing came to my mind. I felt strange and dead, as if I had had a painful shock. Without knowing it, the hurt must have shown in my eyes as Riki, who was watching my face for a sign, suddenly lost control.

"All right," he shouted, "if you are going to look like that, I'll never play with you again. Never! Do you understand? Never!"

My dismay was so complete I let him walk away, leaving me with the feeling that something had broken in the centre of me, and the two parts were moving in opposite directions. I knew I could not live without Riki and I rushed to reassure him, knowing that the painful part, which I did not understand at that time, would have to be hidden. I caught up with him at the Chalet steps where he had joined the other children, but I did not say anything to him, as I found myself drawn into their game.

> "Scions scions scions des bois,
> Pour la mère, pour la mère,
> Scions scions scions des bois,
> Pour la mère Nicola."

We continued singing faster and faster, holding hands with our arms crossed, swinging them up and down, until we came to the last line, whereupon we would shout "YO" and leap into the air. But I was feeling irritable and disturbed, and before we had reached the end of the song, I had pushed someone accidentally, who had pushed me back, and I pushed her hard and she pushed me so that I stumbled; and I pushed her so that she fell over; and then they all turned against me, and they pushed me and shoved me and

found fault and criticised, and they accused me of spoiling everything, and they surrounded me like barking dogs, snapping and fighting. And I tried to stand up against their battling arms and hands to speak out, but their faces were full of hate, and when Riki joined them and spoke angrily at me, I burst into tears and fled from them all.

   I rushed into the Chalet and up the stairs and rested my head against the banisters, and I looked down at the cool stone floor in the quiet of the hall below, and I cried and cried until my eyes were puffed and sore, and I felt ugly and small and of no importance. The wall next to me had shelves full of books right up to the ceiling, so I took a book down and looked at it and thought to myself while I was still crying, "I shall read and read; everything outside the house is a waste. Why should I bother with it at all? I don't care about any of them; they can do what they like. I shall read this book which is something really worth doing, and when I've finished it, I shall read the next one and the next one, and I shall always have something to do, without having to depend on anyone, which will be a good thing." And suddenly, I was huge with a billowing grief that could not find room inside myself to swell and break out and drain away. I looked at the book, but there was a film between me and the print on the page, so I cannot remember now what the book was called, or even if I held it the right way up; and I wondered if the people who read and wrote books did it because something terrible had happened to them. But I pushed that thought away and considered that reading was a very important thing to do.

In the hall I heard the door open and Riki calling me, but I was hot and aching with crying and trying not to cry. I kept still and looking as indifferent as I could I bent over the book, turning a page to show how interested I was in my occupation. Riki came up the stairs still calling, but I pretended I was reading, and had not heard or noticed anything, and when he saw me, he was gentle and pleaded for me to go down and said that it was all his fault. But my pride was so hurt, I could not go out or face anyone again, and I wanted to dwindle and shrink and become small and then invisible, and I hated my swollen, red, sticky, dripping face.

Riki said, "I want you to come down, we all want you to come down." I shuffled the pages of my book and said, "I want to read, I love reading, it's the only thing in the world worth doing," and I was annoyed with myself when the tears started to pour out of my eyes again, and I could

found fault and criticised, and they accused me of spoiling everything, and they surrounded me like barking dogs, snapping and fighting. And I tried to stand up against their battling arms and hands to speak out, but their faces were full of hate, and when Riki joined them and spoke angrily at me, I burst into tears and fled from them all.

    I rushed into the Chalet and up the stairs and rested my head against the banisters, and I looked down at the cool stone floor in the quiet of the hall below, and I cried and cried until my eyes were puffed and sore, and I felt ugly and small and of no importance. The wall next to me had shelves full of books right up to the ceiling, so I took a book down and looked at it and thought to myself while I was still crying, "I shall read and read; everything outside the house is a waste. Why should I bother with it at all? I don't care about any of them; they can do what they like. I shall read this book which is something really worth doing, and when I've finished it, I shall read the next one and the next one, and I shall always have something to do, without having to depend on anyone, which will be a good thing." And suddenly, I was huge with a billowing grief that could not find room inside myself to swell and break out and drain away. I looked at the book, but there was a film between me and the print on the page, so I cannot remember now what the book was called, or even if I held it the right way up; and I wondered if the people who read and wrote books did it because something terrible had happened to them. But I pushed that thought away and considered that reading was a very important thing to do.

In the hall I heard the door open and Riki calling me, but I was hot and aching with crying and trying not to cry. I kept still and looking as indifferent as I could I bent over the book, turning a page to show how interested I was in my occupation. Riki came up the stairs still calling, but I pretended I was reading, and had not heard or noticed anything, and when he saw me, he was gentle and pleaded for me to go down and said that it was all his fault. But my pride was so hurt, I could not go out or face anyone again, and I wanted to dwindle and shrink and become small and then invisible, and I hated my swollen, red, sticky, dripping face.

Riki said, "I want you to come down, we all want you to come down." I shuffled the pages of my book and said, "I want to read, I love reading, it's the only thing in the world worth doing," and I was annoyed with myself when the tears started to pour out of my eyes again, and I could

The Quarrel

not stop them falling although I never made a sound. But I went on pretending to read the pages, which were just a blur. Riki put his arm round me and said, "This is nonsense, Pegee, you must come down and play with us. No one is going to say anything to you about what has happened and anyway, when you're not there, I don't like it any more. So please come down, Pegee, because I love you better than anyone else in the whole world." When he said that, I could not resist any longer and I got up and we went downstairs together.

The children outside were standing about and they did not look at me or notice anything, and their faces were ordinary as if nothing had happened, and they went on talking about what would be the best thing to do next. When somebody remembered the donkey-cart, which was empty and not in use, we all ran to get it. As I was first, they said I could drive while two of them pulled the shafts. So I got on the cart and stood like an Ancient Briton in a chariot, using a rope for reins and, holding a long branch of leaves which I waved in the air, I shouted for them to be off. The wheels trundled over the ground, and all the other children raced beside the cart, screaming and yelling in French or English or whatever their language happened to be. I felt as if I was Boadicea with white horses galloping triumphantly away from the battlefield after defeating the enemy. I felt invincible, as if I could do anything in the whole world. I didn't even mind running over the buttercups and things which normally I would have minded. I felt so high up, it was almost like flying over a mountain. Anyway all the children had a chance to ride in the cart, and pretend they were King or Queen or whatever they imagined themselves to be, and at the end of the day everyone was satisfied and laughing and out of breath.

When Auntie Prissie called us in for supper, the other children left and Dinah and Riki and I went into the dining-room, which was warm with the evening sun. We had

Running Wild

home-made rolls straight from the oven and French chocolate in hot milk. The older girls came home with their friends, and we all started talking at the same time in different languages, so that the words rose and fell in the air with a soft, hard, sweet, sharp, high, low sound until we could not keep our eyes open and were sent to bed.

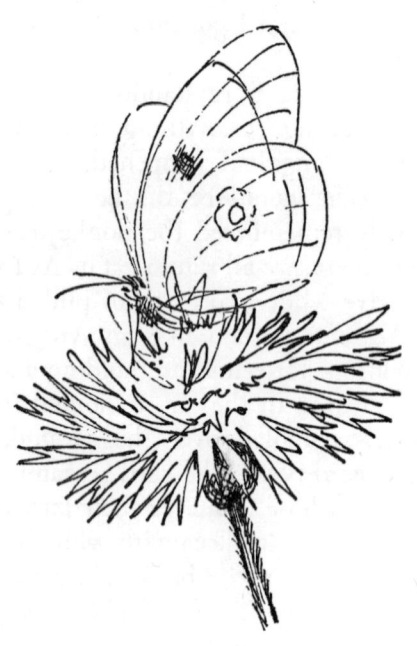

The Poem

I wanted to express my feelings about all the things I saw and felt at this time, but I did not know how to do it. I must have painted some pictures, because I remember Auntie Prissie showing one or two to Monsieur Gil. I was not in the room at the time, but I could see both of them quite clearly through the glass panel in the dining-room door. I remember him putting on a pair of silver-rimmed spectacles and bending over the table to look at them. The spectacles looked strange to me, and wrong, as I always thought of him as a very young man. He was big with brown hair that soared upwards and fell over at the ends. He could not speak English. I could see him saying something to Auntie Prissie, then he lost interest and turned away.

After he had gone Auntie Prissie told me he had said that "he could not draw as well as I could, when he was my age". This compliment did not have a very encouraging effect. I wanted to be told that I had genius, and hoped that I would be looked at with a new interest. This was not conceit, but an idea that nothing but genius would make up for my other inadequacies. After Riki's confession, I felt that loving and being loved was a shifting, unpredictable business that might lead any time to betrayal.

"When I grow up," said Dinah, "I want to make everybody in the whole world envy me, don't you?" I hardly knew how to answer, as I lacked any experience of being envied. People were inclined to ask me why I looked so pale? so tired? so thin? And what a pity my hair, which was such a nice colour, was so straight.

I took refuge in poetry and wrote a particularly long poem about a woman who died of grief when the man she loved was drowned at sea. I remember thinking how surprised everyone would be to discover that I knew all about passion and suffering. I took the poem to Auntie Laura and asked her to give me her opinion. She glanced at it with a little tucked-in smile, put the poem in a drawer without reading it, and said that she would let me know what she thought about it later. Later seemed like years, but I imagine it was only a day or two afterwards that Auntie Laura suggested we should all go for a walk on the dunes.

I remember two things about that calm sunny afternoon and one of them was Casin's studio. We found it in a bird-piping place amongst the gorse. We pushed our way through the overgrown grass to see inside the windows which were partly concealed by boards. The large room seemed full of figures, eyes looking at us, arms held out in gestures of delicate affection or as if to ward us off. Some of the statues were draped in cloth. A pair of feet beneath an old curtain looked like someone hiding. A figure pointed at nowhere in particular. Although I knew they were sculptures, they had a quality which made them look like real people waiting for some remarkable event. We went from window to window to get a better view.

"Casin is dead," said Auntie Laura, "there's nothing to see there now, dears, so don't be long."

She walked away chewing and pouting her mouth, talking silently to someone who wasn't there, while wisps of white hair floated round her head like a little smoke. I was still pushing the undergrowth away from the window hoping to see something more ordinary—a cup on a table, a coat hanging somewhere, a chair, or even a pair of old boots; I needed some other visible sign that someone had lived in this house, someone like me. But there was nothing more, only statues staring at us, like the people in the Greek story who had been turned to stone by some catastrophe, with their white heads looking up or down or over their shoulders.

I cannot imagine why the sight of this house, not at that time so remarkable, should be so remarkably unforgettable. What struck me most was the silence; there was hardly any wind except for the occasional swish in the grass, like someone running away.

The Poem

I turned round to look at Auntie Laura, a little figure nearly as small as me, in a long black cotton mourning dress, and a flat black hat. She looked as if she was nodding to someone as she disappeared down the path. It was all surprisingly clear and light. The air had a luminous quality which gave the effect of a house in a bottle, or one of those glass balls which you shake and snow falls. In this case the glass ball was huge, it encompassed the whole sky which was full of larks, and the snow lay all about inside the house, and was plaster of Paris.

Riki and Dinah were running towards someone in the long grass. I went to see who it was, and found myself looking up at a big bronze statue of a man, standing as if on guard in front of the house.

"That's Casin," said Dinah, "his wife made it just before she died." I was stunned; I tried to think of Casin and his wife being dead, but it was too difficult. The colour of the bronze was dark, and this made him look alive and very solid against the crystal green of the grass, which was full of changing lights from the clouds passing, and his face was framed by a sky the colour of an amethyst.

"What will happen to his things?" I said.

"No one would touch anything that belonged to Casin."

I put my hand on his shoe, which felt smooth and slippery, like real leather. Dressed in neat everyday clothes, he looked a smart, sensible sort of man. "Perhaps," I thought, "that's why it looks so odd, seeing a statue with such an air of respectability, standing miles from anywhere, amongst thistles and thorns, bindweed round his legs, and nothing but grass waving." I had a funny feeling as we walked away, that Casin was watching us, and breathing, and having thoughts about our being there.

"What will happen to the statue?" I said.

"It will stay there for ever and ever."

"What about the house?"

"That too, because he's an artist. It's a kind of memorial."

This was something I could understand. The village people were proud of their artists; they seemed to regard them as labourers like themselves often working for long hours for no money at all. Nevertheless, I regretted leaving him there alone in the grass, with all those people he had made. "Someone," I thought, "should have given each one the right kind of home."

"Casin isn't famous yet, is he?" said Riki.

"Everybody knows about Casin," said Dinah.

"Poor Monsieur Gil can never sell his pictures."

The Poem

"Oh, well, the people here are too poor to buy them, but they take pots of hot food to his house when the weather's cold, and when the summer comes he tries to sell his pictures in Boulogne."

"My father bought a picture from him once," I said. "It was a drawing of my mother on dark pink paper."

"Come on," said Riki, and we rushed to catch up with Auntie Laura.

"I know every inch of this ground," said Auntie Laura, as we joined her, "but I've never given any of these little places a name. Look at that little hollow of sand over there, with all those big stones round it. What shall we call it? Petit Couvert? Petit Cachet? Or what about Grotte de Suite?"

I thought these names were rather tame for wild and lonely places, but anyway I could not wait any longer, and I asked Auntie Laura what she thought about my poem. She looked as if she was sorry I had mentioned it. Her face had a shut-in look, and her mouth began to nibble for words. She did not look at me as she spoke, and she sounded as if she was saying something she had been taught to say by somebody else.

"Yes," she said, "I've read your poem, dear, but you mustn't write about things you don't understand, particularly when you have had no experience of them. Try and write about the things you know."

"What sort of things?" I said, feeling sullen and disappointed.

"Well," she said, pointing to a poppy, "you could probably write a very nice little poem about that."

I felt too humiliated to reply. Riki nudged me. "I expect she showed the poem to Auntie Prissie," he whispered. I looked at Auntie Laura and wondered why, considering she was the nicest of all the aunts, or anyway I thought so, did she have to shuffle about in the shadows keeping out of everybody's way. If only she would take part in what was

happening to us, she might have made Auntie Prissie more sympathetic. It never occurred to me to ask Auntie Laura if she had ever been in love, or lost someone she loved, or if she had ever felt despair; she always looked so old, almost indifferent, wearing those black cobwebby clothes and squashed flat hat, I assumed such matters had passed her by.

When I got back to the Chalet, I dashed off a poem without feeling any emotion at all.

> "Dress of red,
>   Coat of green,
>   This is all that I have seen,
>   But a little tuft of grass
>   Waving, waving as I pass."

The Poem

Then I went and handed it to Auntie Laura. It was meant to show how stupid she was, but she took it quite seriously. "Thank you, dear," she said, "that was very sweet of you." All the same, I could not help wondering why she sounded so weary, just as if she had been defeated in some terrible battle.

"There's really nothing more I can write about a flower, Auntie Laura."

"No, dear," she said, "I don't suppose there is, but there are lots of other little things. Perhaps you'll be able to think of something. One just has to go on trying."

After that I lost all interest in poetry. I did not know what to do; neither did I care very much. I sat a lot of the time in the wicker chair in the hall thinking of nothing. The sky slowly turned grey again, and everything looked dull.

Suddenly, one day through the glass front-door, I saw my sister Niña standing on the steps outside. The wind blew so hard her hair stood straight up in the air, but she was smiling, and all that I had been keeping down and trying to forget came pouring up in a torrent of feeling I could not put into words and stuck in my throat like a large stone. Everyone rushed into the hall to meet her, all talking at once, and Niña had an arm round me as she told everybody how rough the sea had been and, yes, she had been sick and, yes, the boat had rolled and, yes, it was lovely to be back, and she had come to fetch me and, yes, the trip took longer than they thought. I wanted to say something, but the stone in my throat prevented me. I knew that if I opened my mouth I would burst out crying, and everyone would look amazed; so I stood there and smiled, which was all I could manage to do.

"Well!" said Auntie Prissie, "Peggy doesn't seem very pleased to see you. She hasn't even said hallo."

I must have looked a fool, as I did not dare to move, or change my face, or speak. Niña laughed politely but, to my relief, she took no notice of Auntie Prissie. She said

Running Wild

afterwards she knew how I felt, and she went on talking about our mother, and the sea, and Derek coming on later; but her arm was round me all the time, and as she did not ask me anything, or expect me to talk, I recovered quite quickly.

When we had left the Chalet it was quite wonderful walking down the hill together, both of us talking at the same time. I no longer felt like a stone or a lifeless kind of statue. Niña told me how she had felt on the sea with a gale blowing ... and how much drawing she couldn't do ... and her fiancé who was meeting her soon ... and the blue-eyed steward who had put a rug round her as she had preferred to stay on deck ... and our mother who was waiting ... and Daddy had liked my last poem ... and we were all sleeping in the same rooms ... and wasn't the weather wonderful? We could all go bathing now. I never realised until that moment how much I had got to talk about. I felt as free as the wind.

The Picnic

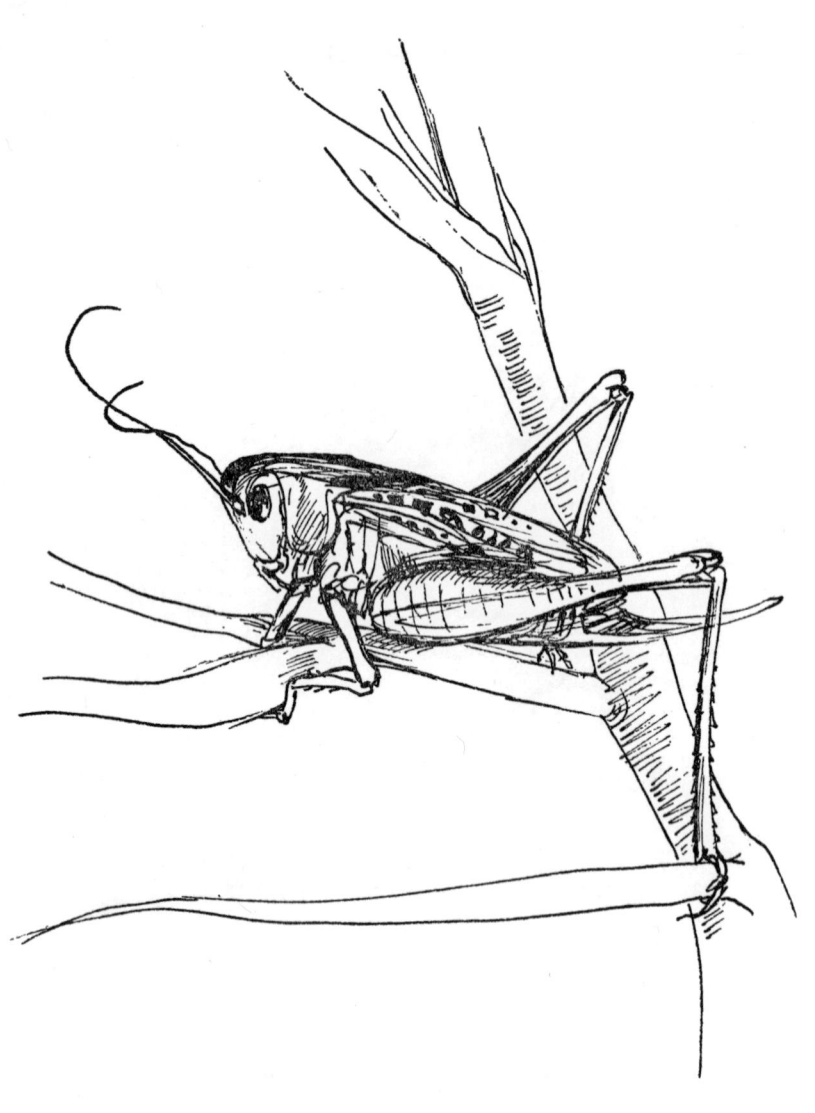

At the end of our last summer holiday in France we went for a picnic in a forest, near the sea, quite a long way from the village, but I cannot remember the name of the place. I can only remember the feel of the day, and a car standing in the road ready to kick up the dust. Although it was early, the heat was coming in waves, everyone fanned themselves with papers or hats. Tessa, who was responsible for the day being planned, pointed out that most of the others had gone in the first two cars so, swaying like a tree under her Japanese sunshade, she waved us all into the back of the last car, wondering whether we would fit. My mother was doubtful, having arrived, she said, "for the purpose of calling." But Tessa smiled, and said we were all expected. The only person she could not find was Riki, and thought he might have gone with the Aunts to Boulogne. At that my heart sank, and I did not care about the picnic, or the car, or the sun which felt black, heavy and intolerable, and I felt as dry as the dust. I was so much in love with Riki that to be separated from him on what promised to be the day of days was a disappointment I could hardly endure.

"Riki might have gone in the last car," said Tessa, looking at me. But guessing was worse, and the drive was a nightmare. The hood was down, and there was enough breeze to make us all look like bundles of flags, with so many chiffon scarves and ribbons flowing backwards; everyone was out for a good time, except me. I could hardly wait until we got there: it might have been night for all I cared.

We stopped in the middle of a great pine-wood where the trees were straight and cool. The ground was red with pine-needles and undulated like waves and the fir-cones lying about were as big as foxes' tails. Suddenly I saw Riki running down the slope calling my name over and over. The sun soared and everything leapt about inside me as we all poured out of the car, and Riki and I stood and looked at each other and smiled. I cannot remember the details: it all turned into a fuzzy snapshot—someone in a cloche hat was sitting on the hood holding a camera, as we clambered up the hill to take up our positions.

We children ran off to play in the wood. Lovers lay in the shadows. The older ones put up their parasols and talked, or lay with their faces under handkerchiefs and went to sleep. My mother, who was in a rose silk heat-wave dress and holding a panama sunshade, reminded us of dangers, such as wasps, and going too close or going too far, but she was soon talking to someone else and moving towards the trees where people were meeting each other.

Tessa was counting the cups, and a table was laid as if we were in a huge drawing-room with plumped-up sofas which were really hillocks of red pine-needles as soft as plush to sit on, and the trees like pillars holding up the roof. Everyone had a silver spoon to stir their coffee, and moustaches of cream and crumbs were wiped away with napkins tied round the neck. There were home-made scones and bubbly water in bottles which I rather liked. The sea was further than usual, but sighing a little all the time so that we knew it was there.

There were crowds of children, but Riki and I wandered away to sit amongst the grass inside a circle of bushes, to talk about being old and married. Soon I was to leave him, being eleven next birthday, and going to a new school.

"Remember," he said, "remember, only you and only me ..."

Even the grass seemed to promise, as he tied a green blade round my finger like a ring.

"That means you, and that means me, never," he said, "never ..." and looked so solemn, that I had to promise never to marry anyone else; but even as I said it, I knew something was approaching that would divide us, but what it was I did not know. I told him that the grass on my finger would die. I wanted gold: I thought I ought to have a real

The Picnic

ring. Something must be done, I said, to join us for ever, or we would never meet again. Riki looked about him and could not find anything, and said that he had not got a ring, and not knowing what to do next, he leant forward and kissed me on the mouth and said that was "for all time". In the end we lay on the grass and looked at the branches of the trees which were like ladders leading to the sky, and I felt soft and at ease and as warm as the ground I was lying on, until I heard Riki being called.

"Never forget," were the last words I heard as we tore out of the bushes into the air where I must have lost my grass leaf ring, as our flight was stopped by his pale-faced mama in her snow-coloured dress, who caught him as he was flying past her. "Say goodbye," she said to him, for she was always coming and going, and he was proud as he talked to her, boasting and laughing having her for a whole minute of his life, although she had almost orphaned him. We watched her walk away, blowing kisses, lisping French words, waving to us amongst the trees like a cabbage butterfly as she fluttered off, and Riki was fat with pride at having a parent to show me.

Someone arrived after that and took us for a walk, or did we go alone? Anyway, there was a path leading to a garden right in the heart of the wood, where the shrubs moved back to let us pass as we pushed our way towards a little church, as small as a house, smelling of incense, with velvety-black scented gates. We clung to the warm bars looking in to the darkness, which was deep red, being lit by one light. "This must be a home for sweethearts," I thought, as we rattled the gates, but they would not open.

"There's another way in," said Riki, so guided by the sound of bees we followed the path round the church, and there at the back lay a whole garden humming in front of us. In the centre was a lily-pond which shivered with insects and fish nosing about amongst the water-lily leaves.

The Picnic

There was nothing we wanted to do then but run all round it. As we ran everything seemed to be moving quickly past me, as if I was standing still and watching it all. We raced down crazy paths, under arches of leaves, through long tunnels of roses and ivy, up flights of steps, over bridges of stone, down the slopes and along the paths again. Clusters of flowers burst as if they were blazing on each side of us in kaleidoscopic patterns of wine, rose, peach, pink, scarlet, crimson, deep dark burgundy; gold lay all over the leaves from the sun and masses of blue and white flowers rose like smoke between a fire of blossoms where each petal was like a pointed flame. At last Riki and I were too hot to run any more and sat panting near the pond. We dipped our fingers in the thick weedy water where the fish rose to the surface with open mouths. It was so quiet that we could hear bubbles popping and gnats sawing up and down in the air.

In the distance we heard voices calling; and the garden retreated in a haze of heat as we walked away from it. I looked back at the lily-pond where the fishes fanned themselves in the deep brown water, and the water-lilies rose like wax stars out of the bottom of the pond.

"Maybe it's just a dream," I said to Riki.

"Yes," said Riki, "but come on Pegee or we'll never get away."

We went down the path and into the wood again where it was cool after the hot sun, and the trees were still and silent as if they had been painted. "It's like moving through a picture," I thought.

"It's our garden," said Riki, "next year we'll come back and see it again."

But I was doubtful about coming back to France, and I tried to tell Riki about the new school, with the gymnasium which had ropes like creepers hanging from the ceiling, and the pool where I would learn to swim; but Riki did not want to hear.

"I don't want you to go, Pegee," he said.

So I hugged him, and reminded him that he would soon be living with his mother again, and Riki smiled and said, "We will all be happy then." And he pointed at the road and shouted, "There they are!" We ran through the trees, where everyone had gathered, as they said a storm was coming, and all the cars were ready to take us home.

Such a commotion was made with packing and putting up the hoods, that they could not understand what we were telling them. Veronica denied the existence of the church but remembered a garden. Gwyneth remembered the church, but said the garden was just some old graveyard near a ditch, where the flowers were running wild; and Bronya said that we had invented it all, and she laughed at us mischievously. But Tessa, who was busy counting everyone, said impatiently, yes, she had seen the church, and yes, it was in a garden, and both of them were absolutely real, and she advised us to hurry and get in the car before it rained.

High up in the sky, the wind had started to sing in a thin but wild sort of way; and a clump of grass swished suddenly like someone tossing back their hair. As soon as we got inside the car, the rain poured down making a noise like thunder on the canvas hood, and everyone started talking and laughing at the same time, looking inside their baskets and handbags to see if they had forgotten anything, as we all drove home over the hills.

"It's been a lovely day, hasn't it?" my mother said to me, "and look! the rain is passing, the clouds are moving away."

Suddenly I felt as if I could not wait to get out of my childhood. It seemed as if something was coming that was bigger and better than anything that had been before, and it made me feel excited, like seeing a radiant, rainbow-coloured landscape through a rent in a cloud before a mist rolled over it again.

The Picnic

"I will come and see you off on the boat," said Riki, when we left him at the Chalet.

And he did. The last sight I had of him was from the bow of a ship, as I watched him break away from Auntie Prissie, and run along the wharf beside the ship, right to the very end where he stood waving and waving until he disappeared behind the waves.

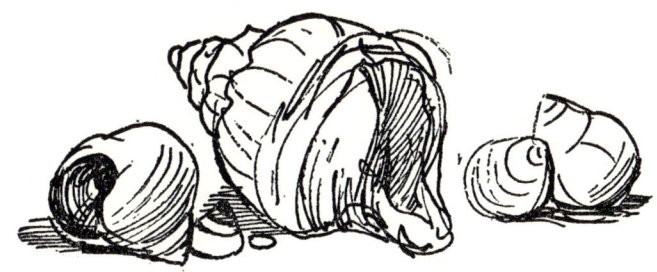